Collins

Year 1
Maths & English
Targeted Study
& Practice Book

Jon Goulding and Brad Thompson

How to use this book

This Maths and English Study and Practice book contains everything children need for the school year in one book.

A **study page** and a **practice page** for each topic.

Tips give ideas on how to remember key information.

'**Remember**' boxes highlight key points

Key words highlighted on each Study page with definitions in the glossary.

Questions split into three levels of difficulty – **Challenge 1**, **Challenge 2** and **Challenge 3** – to help progression.

Total marks boxes for recording progress and '**How am I doing**' checks for self-evaluation.

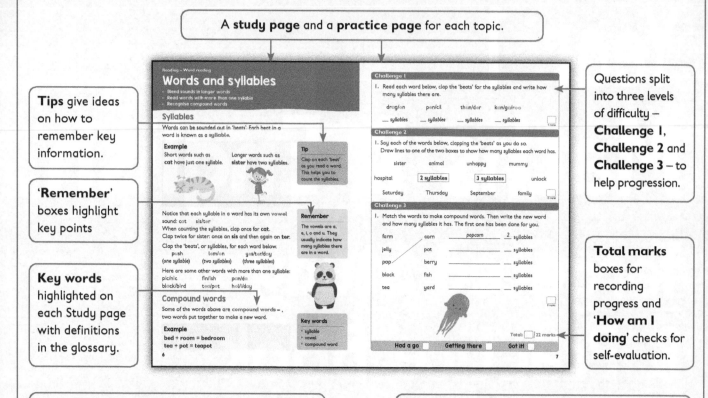

Four **Progress tests** included throughout the book for ongoing assessment and monitoring progress.

Mixed questions for maths and English test topics from throughout the book.

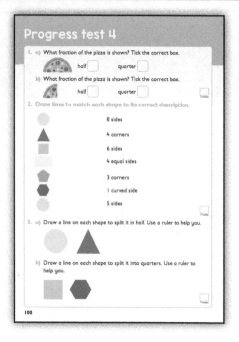

Problem-solving questions identified with a clear symbol.

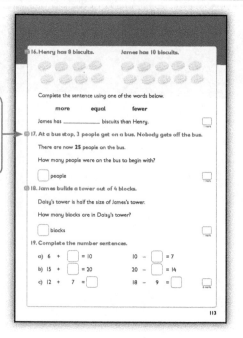

Answers provided for all the questions.

Contents

Sounds and words

- Recognise different sounds for letters
- Blend sounds to read unfamiliar words

Different sounds

The 26 **letters** in the alphabet are used to make 44 different **sounds**.

Example

s can make the sound in **s**at

h can make the sound in **h**at

Together as **sh** they make the sound in **sh**op and fi**sh**.

Remember

Some letters can make different sounds when used with other letters.

When sounds are written down, letters or groups of letters are used to represent the sounds. s, h, c, sh and ch are all sounds written down.

When reading **words**, the sounds represented by the letters are put together. This is known as **blending** sounds.

Tip

Read the rest of the words in a sentence if you are unsure of a word. It might help you to work it out.

Example

cot has three letters and three sounds: **c o t**

eat has three letters and two sounds: **ea t**

Blending the sounds together helps you to say the word.

Look at the words below and say each sound. Blend the sounds together to read each word.

ch ea t ⟶ cheat   g r ow ⟶ grow
sh u t ⟶ shut   s t ea l ⟶ steal
r i ng ⟶ ring   t r a p ⟶ trap
l u n ch ⟶ lunch   b ir th ⟶ birth
p i ck ⟶ pick   s p r ay ⟶ spray

Key words

- letter
- sound
- word

Challenge 1

1. Sound out and then blend each word.
   Circle each real word.

   p ie   sh ir t   g ea p

   h a ng   p l ay   b r oy

   4 marks

Challenge 2

1. a) Circle the words with **two** sounds.

   chips   **if**   **up**   **eat**

   b) Circle the words with **three** sounds.

   tick   **dog**   **shut**   **no**

   6 marks

Challenge 3

1. Use the words below to complete the sentences.

   bunch   **sting**   **soap**   **Throw**

   a) Wash your hands with _____.

   b) _____ the ball.

   c) A _____ of flowers.

   d) A bee can _____.

   4 marks

   Total: ☐/14 marks

   Had a go ☐   Getting there ☐   Got it! ☐

5

Words and syllables

- Blend sounds in longer words
- Read words with more than one syllable
- Recognise compound words

Syllables

Words can be sounded out in 'beats'. Each beat in a word is known as a **syllable**.

Example

Short words such as **cat** have just one syllable.

Longer words such as **sister** have two syllables.

Notice that each syllable in a word has its own **vowel** sound: cat   sis/ter

When counting the syllables, clap once for **cat**.

Clap twice for sister: once on **sis** and then again on **ter**.

Clap the 'beats', or syllables, for each word below.

    push   lem/on   yes/ter/day
(one syllable)   *(two syllables)*   *(three syllables)*

Here are some other words with more than one syllable:

pic/nic   fin/ish   pan/da
black/bird   tea/pot   hol/i/day

Compound words

Some of the words above are **compound words** – two words put together to make a new word.

Example

bed + room = bedroom

tea + pot = teapot

1. Read each word below, clap the 'beats' for the syllables and write how many syllables there are.

drag/on   pen/cil   thun/der   kan/ga/roo

__ syllables   __ syllables   __ syllables   __ syllables

4 marks

1. Say each of the words below, clapping the 'beats' as you do so.
   Draw lines to one of the two boxes to show how many syllables each word has.

sister   animal   unhappy   mummy

hospital   **2 syllables**   **3 syllables**   unlock

Saturday   Thursday   September   family

10 marks

1. Match the words to make compound words. Then write the new word and how many syllables it has. The first one has been done for you.

farm   corn   _popcorn_   2 syllables

jelly   pot   _____   __ syllables

pop   berry   _____   __ syllables

black   fish   _____   __ syllables

tea   yard   _____   __ syllables

8 marks

Total: [   ] / 22 marks

Had a go [ ]   **Getting there** [ ]   **Got it!** [ ]

Suffixes

- Know that different endings can be added to words
- Read words ending in -s, -es, -er, -est, -ed and -ing

Adding a suffix

Words can be changed slightly by adding a different ending, known as a **suffix**.

Adding **-s** or **-es** changes a word from **singular** (one) to **plural** (more than one).

Tip

Use picture clues to help you see if there is more than one.

Example

Here is a banana.

Here are three banana**s**.

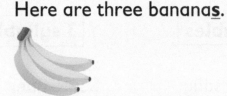

Here is a fox.

Here are two fox**es**.

Adding **-es** adds an extra syllable: **fox** has one syllable, **foxes** has two.

-s can make a 's' sound as in <u>s</u>at or a 'z' sound as in <u>z</u>ebra.

| socks | weeks | cups | cats | ← -s makes a 's' sound |
| cars | dogs | pens | mugs | ← -s makes a 'z' sound |

Adding **-er, -est, -ed** or **-ing** also adds an extra syllable.

-er	-est
farm – farm**er** fast – fast**er**	great – great**est** slow – slow**est**
-ed	**-ing**
post – post**ed** lift – lift**ed**	walk – walk**ing** think – think**ing**

Remember

In some words, the final letter is doubled when a suffix is added, e.g. run ⟶ run**n**ing.

Adding **-ed** does not always add an extra syllable but the **-ed** ending can sound different for different words:

jump**ed** [a 't' sound]   stay**ed** [a 'd' sound]   wait**ed** [an 'id' sound]

Key words

- suffix
- singular
- plural

8

1. Write the plural of each singular word.

egg ⇨ _____   **house** ⇨ _____   **chip** ⇨ _____

book ⇨ _____   **bird** ⇨ _____

5 marks

1. Tick the correct word to complete each sentence.

I am the   **greater.** ☐   I am the   **slowest.** ☐
           greatest. ☐   **slower.** ☐

I am   **runner.** ☐   I am a   **farming.** ☐
           running. ☐   **farmer.** ☐

4 marks

1. Read each word with an **-ed** ending. Draw a line to show whether it has a 't' sound, a 'd' sound or an 'id' sound at the end.

't' sound   **'d' sound**   **'id' sound**

   pointed   punched   played

3 marks

Total: ☐ /12 marks

Had a go ☐   **Getting there** ☐   **Got it!** ☐

Common exception words

- **Read exception words**

Some things are not as they seem!

Some words cannot be sounded out because the letters do not make the sound they usually make. These words are **exception words**, which just have to be learned.

Example

<u>You</u> have a book.   It is <u>your</u> book. It is <u>our</u> book.

In the sentences above, **ou** makes a different sound in each underlined word.

The **'ere'** in h**ere**, th**ere** and wh**ere** can also be tricky.

Example

H**ere** is the dog.
Wh**ere** is the rabbit?
Th**ere** is the cat.

In the sentences above, **ere** makes a different sound in **here** to the sound it makes in **where** and **there**.

Double letters

Short words ending in 'l' or 's' usually have the final letter doubled at the end.

Example

pu**ll** ti**ll** wi**ll** fu**ll**   ki**ss** mi**ss** me**ss** fu**ss**

But there are exceptions, such as:
pal
bus

Challenge 1

1. Draw lines to match each incorrect word on the left to its correct spelling on the right.

a) sed   friend

b) pul   pull

c) skool   said

d) frend   school

Challenge 2

1. Choose the correct word to replace the incorrect underlined word in each sentence, and write it in the space given.

loved   **Once**   **One**   **some**

a) Wons upon a time there was a cat. _____

b) The cat had sum kittens.   _____

c) She luved them.   _____

d) Won kitten ate fish.   _____

Challenge 3

1. Underline the correct word in each pair below.

Jeff **waz / was** a farmer. He **iz / is** now a **buss / bus** driver.

His / hiz shirt **has / haz** green spots. Soon **hee / he** **will / wil**

be / bee at home.

Total: ____ /16 marks

Had a go ☐   Getting there ☐   Got it! ☐

Apostrophes

- Recognise when two words have been joined together
- Understand that an apostrophe represents missing letters

Apostrophes for missing letters

When we want to push two words together to make a shorter word, a letter or letters are left out and replaced with an **apostrophe**. These words are called **contractions**. We make words shorter so that they are easier to say.

Example

You will love the cake.

You and **will** can be pushed together:

You~will~   ← [w and i are removed]

w and **i** are replaced with an apostrophe:

You'll love the cake.

Remember

The apostrophe goes where the letters were.

Remember

Y o u ' l l

↑

This is what the apostrophe looks like.

Here are some other contractions:

- **They will** play football. → **They'll** play football.

- **We are** going on holiday. → **We're** going on holiday.

- **I have** got to go home. → **I've** got to go home.

- She **did not** like the clown. → She **didn't** like the clown.

- **She is** happy today. → **She's** happy today.

Tip

Think about how you say contracted words in everyday speech. It will help you remember how to say them when you are reading.

Key words

- apostrophe
- contraction

1. Draw lines to match the words to their shortened version.

a) we have   I'm

b) I am   they'll

c) they will   aren't

d) are not   we've

4 marks

1. Circle the correct shortened word that could replace the underlined words in each sentence.

a) He <u>did not</u> know what time it was.   **didn't / don't**

b) <u>You are</u> going to be late.   **You've / You're**

c) <u>They are</u> not for sale.   **They're / They'll**

d) This <u>is not</u> the right place.   **isn't / aren't**

4 marks

1. Read the sentences. Write the **long form** of the underlined contractions in the space provided.

a) The dogs <u>can't</u> go in the living room. _____

b) Their car <u>shouldn't</u> make that noise. _____

c) Tomorrow <u>we're</u> making soup. _____

d) I think <u>I've</u> got a cold. _____

4 marks

Total: ___ /12 marks

Had a go ☐   **Getting there** ☐   **Got it!** ☐

13

Fiction texts

- Understand what a fiction text is
- Recognise key events and predictable phrases

Fiction

A **fiction** text is a made-up story. Traditional tales and fairytales such as *Goldilocks and the Three Bears* and *Cinderella* are fiction texts.

The story title often tells you what or who the story is about. A story has a **beginning**, **middle** and **end**.

Example

Beginning	→	**Middle**	→	**End**
Three bears go out.		Goldilocks goes into their house.		Three bears return and chase Goldilocks away.

Stories often have words, phrases and **structures** that repeat. In *Goldilocks and the Three Bears*, Goldilocks tries different chairs, porridge and beds, with the third one being 'just right'. The three bears say, 'Who's been…', 'eating my porridge?', 'sitting in my chair?', 'sleeping in my bed?'.

Understanding the story

Understanding a story is known as **comprehension**.

Example

A girl was skipping through the woods. She wore a red coat with a hood. Her name was Little Red Riding Hood. On her arm was a basket of food and in her hand were some flowers. Behind a tree stood a wolf. He licked his lips.

From this small part of the story you can answer a number of questions, for example:

Who are the characters?   A girl and a wolf.

What is the girl carrying?   A basket and flowers.

Challenge 1

1. Draw lines to match the characters to the story titles.

Jack and the Beanstalk	The Smartest Giant in Town	Puss in Boots	The Little Red Hen

A giant	A hen	A cat	A boy called Jack

4 marks

Challenge 2

1. Read or listen to the passage and then answer the questions.

Jim and Jess saw the dragon. Its head poked out of the cave. Smoke came from its nose as it snored. Green scales covered its head. If the children wanted the magical treasure, they would have to creep quietly. Jess was scared of the dragon but Jim was scared of the dark and what else they might find in the cave.

a) Who are the main characters? _____

b) Where is the dragon? _____

c) What colour is the dragon? _____

d) How do we know the dragon is sleeping? _____

4 marks

Challenge 3

1. What might be a good title for the story in Challenge 2? Why?

_____

_____

2 marks

Total: ☐ /10 marks

Had a go ☐   **Getting there** ☐   **Got it!** ☐

Poetry

- Explain and discuss understanding of poems
- Respond to poetry

What is a poem?

A **poem** is a type of writing that describes something or tells a story. Poems often have words that **rhyme**.

Example

In the deep blue **sea**,

Live sharks swimming **free**,

In the deep blue **sea**,

Treasure under lock and **key**,

In the deep blue **sea**,

Is mermaid Belle, aged **three**,

In the deep blue **sea**,

It's amazing, you must **agree**.

In this poem, the words at the end of every other line all rhyme with 'sea'.

In the poem above, the words 'In the deep blue sea' are **repeated** several times. Lots of poems contain repeating words, which make the poem fun to join in with and make it easier to remember.

Understanding a poem

It is important to try to understand a poem as you read it.

Example

Humpty Dumpty sat on a wall,

It's about a character called Humpty Dumpty.

Humpty Dumpty had **a great fall**.

Humpty falls.

All the **king's horses** and all the **king's men**,

The king's men (maybe soldiers) on horses come.

Couldn't put Humpty together again.

They could not make Humpty better.

1. Draw lines to join the pairs of rhyming words.

zoo   shore   said   chip   foxes   money

honey   bed   boxes   store   you   ship

6 marks

Challenge 2

1. Read or listen to the poem then answer the questions.

> Jack and Jill,
> Went up the hill,
> To fetch a pail of water.
> Jack fell down,
> And broke his crown,
> And Jill came tumbling after.

a) Who is this poem about? _____

b) Where are they going? _____

c) What are they doing? _____

d) Which word is used to rhyme with Jill? _____

4 marks

Challenge 3

1. Read or listen to the poem in Challenge 2 and then answer the questions.

a) What do you think a 'pail' is? _____

b) What could 'crown' mean in this poem? _____

c) What word is used to show how Jill fell? _____

3 marks

Total: ☐ /13 marks

Had a go ☐   Getting there ☐   Got it! ☐

Non-fiction

- Recognise key features of non-fiction texts

Non-fiction texts

Non-fiction texts are about something real. They contain information about real things.

Example

Here is a non-fiction text with some of its features explained.

Remember

Non-fiction texts are not made-up. They can be about anything at all.

Trees

Trees can be different shapes. Some are big and some are small. They have leaves or needles. They also have a trunk and branches.

Wood, which comes from tree trunks, is used in many different ways.

Title – what the text is about

Pictures to help the reader to understand

Text giving facts and information

Reading a non-fiction text can help you find out information and explain something new.

Example

From reading the text above about trees, you can answer questions, giving information that you have found out.

Are all trees the same?	No, some are big, some are small. There are different shapes and sizes.
Do all trees have leaves?	No, some have needles.
Where does wood come from?	Tree trunks.

Key word

- non-fiction

Challenge 1

1. Draw lines to match each non-fiction book title to the content.

How to Draw	*Woodland Animals*	*Cooking at Home*	*Sailing the World*
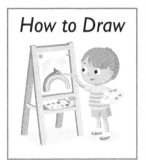			

recipes   **instructions**   **life at sea**   **wildlife**

4 marks

Challenge 2

1. Read the passage from a book called 'Sam's Farm' and then answer the questions.

> Sam is a farmer. He has three hundred cows. The cows are milked each day. The milk is taken away to a dairy. At the dairy, it is put into containers. The milk is then sold in shops.

a) What is the text about? _____

b) What is the name of the farmer? _____

c) What happens to the cows each day? _____

3 marks

Challenge 3

1. Which of these fact boxes works best with the passage in Challenge 2 above? Why?

You probably have milk on your breakfast cereal.	Sam lives in Scotland.	Sheep also live on a farm.

2 marks

_____

_____

Total: [ ] /9 marks

Had a go [ ]   **Getting there** [ ]   **Got it!** [ ]

Inference and prediction

- Make inferences based on what happens in the text
- Make predictions based on what you have read so far

What do you think is happening?

When you are reading, you make **inferences** about the writing based on what happens in the text. This means coming up with ideas about why things happen, or about characters' feelings based on hints that are given in the text.

Example

Jess smiled.

> The word smiled shows that Jess was happy.

Avi frowned. It was time to go shopping.

> The word frowned shows that Avi does not want to go.

What do you think will happen?

When reading, it can be fun to try to think about what might happen next in the story. This is called **prediction**.

Example

The giant chased Jack as he climbed down the beanstalk. When Jack got to the bottom, his mum chopped down the beanstalk.

> You might predict that the beanstalk and the giant come crashing to the ground.

Prince Duncan waited. If anyone could rescue him from the terrible dragon, he would give a great reward. Later, a young lady called Esme came riding through the valley on her horse.

> You might predict that Esme fights the dragon and rescues Prince Duncan. She gets a reward.

Tip

Picking up on hints in the text (making inferences) helps you to understand the story.

Remember

Think about what has happened already to help you think about what might happen next.

Key words

- inference
- prediction

Challenge 1

1. Draw lines to match each picture to the word describing how the character feels.

tired   **upset**   **surprised**   **poorly**   **happy**

5 marks

Challenge 2

1. Read or listen to the text and answer the question.

> The bears saw a hole in the tree. Bees were flying in and out. Daddy bear guessed there would be yummy honey in the hole. Mummy bear banged on the tree with a big stick. Lots of bees came buzzing out of the hole. Baby bear ran away and hid.

Why do you think baby bear hid?

_____

1 mark

Challenge 3

1. Read or listen to the text and answer the questions.

> Dina looked at the box. Her heart was beating fast. She had wanted a puppy for as long as she could remember.
>
> She bit her lip. She wanted to shout with joy but she knew she needed to be quiet. Slowly, she reached into the box.

a) How do you think Dina is feeling? Which words tell you this?

2 marks

_____

b) What do you think will happen next?

_____

1 mark

Total: [ ] / 9 marks

Had a go [ ]   **Getting there** [ ]   **Got it!** [ ]

Progress test 1

1. **Answer the questions about sounds.**

   a) Circle the words with **two** sounds.

   the   **sad**   **on**   **at**

   b) Circle the words with **three** sounds.

   but   **how**   **duck**   **load**

   5 marks

2. **Draw lines to match the words to make compound words, then write the new word and how many syllables it has. The first one has been done for you.**

   post   ground   _playground_   _2_ syllables

   pan   fall   _____   __ syllables

   play   man   _____   __ syllables

   water   cake   _____   __ syllables

   6 marks

3. **Circle the correct word in each pair below.**

   Milly **has / haz** a cat. It **is / iz** called Tom. **Hiz / His** fur is black and white. Soon Tom **wil / will** **be / bee** **one / won** year old.

   6 marks

4. **Circle the correct contraction that could replace the underlined words in each sentence.**

   a) <u>I am</u> nearly ready.   **I'm / I've**

   b) We <u>did not</u> see the film.   **didn't / don't**

   c) <u>We are</u> on the way.   **We'll / We're**

   d) <u>They are</u> not very happy.   **They're / They'll**

   4 marks

5. Read or listen to the text and then answer the questions.

Eva and Grandad went to the park. Grandad had some old bread. Eva broke it into small pieces. They threw the bread into the pond. The ducks came and ate it.

a) Who are the main characters? _____

b) Where did they go? _____

c) What did they do there? _____

d) What word describes the bread? _____

e) Why do you think Eva broke the bread into small pieces?

_____

5 marks

6. Match each word to a word it rhymes with. The first one has been done for you.

hit   boat   red   peel   hot   meat

vote   bit   feet   spot   said   real

5 marks

23

7. Read or listen to the poem then answer the questions.

Little Bo Peep,
Has lost her sheep,
And doesn't know where to find them.

Leave them alone,
And they will come home,
Dragging their tails behind them.

a) Who is this poem about?

_____

b) What problem does she have?

_____

c) Which word is used to rhyme with Peep?

_____

d) What does the poet think will happen if the sheep are left alone?

_____

4 marks

8. Read or listen to the text and answer the questions.

Bees are very important. They live in a hive
and each day they visit lots of flowers.

The bees like the bright colours of the flowers.
They collect nectar and turn it into honey.

Bees help seeds to be made in the flowers.
Seeds are needed to grow new plants.

a) Where do bees live?

_____

b) What do bees make?

_____

c) What are needed to grow new plants?

_____

d) What do the bees collect from flowers?

_____

4 marks

9. Read the sentences. Write the long form of each contraction in the space provided.

a) <u>They'll</u> be ready soon.   _____

b) You <u>can't</u> go in there.   _____

c) We <u>aren't</u> here for long.   _____

d) Tell me when <u>you've</u> finished.   _____

4 marks

10. Add -s or -es to these words to make them plural. Write the plural form of the word.

a) pen   _____

b) arch   _____

c) apple   _____

d) six   _____

4 marks

Total: [   ] / 47 marks

Numbers 1 to 20

- Read and write numbers from 1 to 20

Numerals

A number is used to count something, to find out how many there are.

A **numeral** is how we write a number.

Example

Here is a tennis ball.

There is **1** tennis ball.

1 is the number or numeral.

When **1** is written as a word, it looks like this: **one**

1	2	3	4	5

One	Two	Three	Four	Five

Here are the numbers 1 to 20 in a grid. Each number is written as a word as well.

1	2	3	4	5
one	two	three	four	five
6	7	8	9	10
six	seven	eight	nine	ten
11	12	13	14	15
eleven	twelve	thirteen	fourteen	fifteen
16	17	18	19	20
sixteen	seventeen	eighteen	nineteen	twenty

1. Complete the table. Count the number of objects and write the numeral and word in the columns.

Numeral	Objects	Word

6 marks

1. Someone has jumbled up the letters in these words. They are the words for the numbers **11**, **12**, **13** and **14**.
   Unscramble the words by writing them on the line. Then write the numeral for the word.

   a) routefen   _____   _____

   b) neelev   _____   _____

   c) neethirt   _____   _____

   d) elvtew   _____   _____

4 marks

1. Here is a chart for the numbers 1 to 20. Fill in the missing numerals and words.

1	2	3	4	5
6	7	8	9	10
eleven	twelve	thirteen	fourteen	fifteen
sixteen	seventeen	eighteen	nineteen	twenty

20 marks

Total: ☐ /30 marks

Had a go ☐   **Getting there** ☐   **Got it!** ☐

To 100 and beyond!

- Count forwards and backwards from any number
- Identify one more and one less
- Count to 100

Counting

Counting is a way of finding an amount called the **total**. We show the total with a number.

Each number follows an **order** or sequence.

Example

An empty egg box has 0 eggs in it. If an egg is put in, there is 1 egg. If one more egg is put in, there are 2 eggs. If an egg is put in until the box is full, then there are 6 eggs in the box.

The sequence for filling the egg box is: 0, 1, 2, 3, 4, 5, 6

If an egg is then taken out of the full egg box, there is one less, so there are 5 eggs. If an egg is taken out until the box is empty, then there are 0 eggs.

The sequence for emptying the egg box is: 6, 5, 4, 3, 2, 1, 0

Remember

Counting forwards by 1 each time will give a bigger total. Counting backwards by 1 each time will give a smaller total.

This is counting **forwards**. Each time an egg is put in, the total gets bigger.

This is counting **backwards**. Each time an egg is taken out, the total gets smaller.

Counting to 100

Starting at 0, you can count to 100 by continually adding 1. Look at the **number square**.

Start at 0 and read the numbers in order by adding 1 each time. Then start at 100 and count back to 0.

0	1	2	3	4	5	6	7	8	9	10
11	12	13	14	15	16	17	18	19	20
21	22	23	24	25	26	27	28	29	30
31	32	33	34	35	36	37	38	39	40
41	42	43	44	45	46	47	48	49	50
51	52	53	54	55	56	57	58	59	60
61	62	63	64	65	66	67	68	69	70
71	72	73	74	75	76	77	78	79	80
81	82	83	84	85	86	87	88	89	90
91	92	93	94	95	96	97	98	99	100

Tip

Look for patterns in the number square. What do you notice about the numbers that are underneath each other?

Key words

- ordering
- number square

Challenge 1

Use this number grid to help you count forwards and backwards.

0	1	2	3	4	5	6	7	8	9	10
	11	12	13	14	15	16	17	18	19	20

1. Start at 0 and count forwards the given amounts:

   a) Count on 1 = ☐   b) Count on 3 = ☐   c) Count on 7 = ☐

2. Start at 20 and count backwards the given amounts:

   a) Count back 1 = ☐   b) Count back 4 = ☐   c) Count back 8 = ☐

☐ 6 marks

Challenge 2

1. Fill in the missing numbers in the grid.

21	22	23	24	25	26	27		29	30
31	32		34	35	36	37	38		40
41	42	43		45	46	47	48	49	

☐ 5 marks

Challenge 3

1. Fill in the missing numbers on the number lines.

a)

60 61 62 63 64 65 66 ☐ 68 69 70

b)

80 81 82 83 84 ☐ 86 87 88 89 90

c)
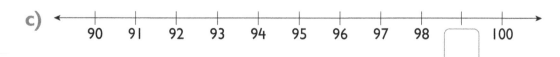
90 91 92 93 94 95 96 97 98 ☐ 100

☐ 3 marks

Total: ☐ / 14 marks

Had a go ☐   **Getting there** ☐   **Got it!** ☐

Twos, fives and tens

- Count in multiples of twos, fives and tens
- Count, read and write numbers to 100

Counting in twos

When counting in steps of two, **add two** each time.

Example

There are **2** mangoes in a pack. When another pack is added, there are **4** mangoes in total. When another pack is added, there are **6** mangoes in total. This is **repeated addition** of 2.

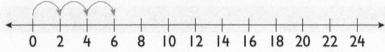

Counting in fives

When counting in steps of five, add **five** each time.

Example

There are **5** apples on a tray. When another tray is added, there are **10** apples in total. When another tray is added, there are **15** apples in total. This is **repeated addition** of 5.

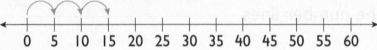

Counting in tens

When counting in steps of ten, add **ten** each time.

Example

There are **10** satsumas in a pack. When another pack is added, there are **20** satsumas in total. When another pack is added, there are **30** satsumas in total. This is **repeated addition** of 10.

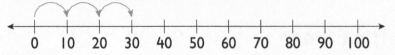

Remember

Counting forwards by 2, 5 or 10 is much quicker than counting in ones.

Tip

Look for twos, fives and tens in everyday objects, such as a pair of socks (2), the fingers on gloves (5), a pack of pencils (10).

Key words

- addition
- repeated addition

Use the number lines on the opposite page to help you answer the questions.

Challenge 1

1. Count the objects and write the totals.

a) [ ] socks

b) [ ] mittens

2. Continue the number sequence, counting in steps of 2.

0   2   [ ]   [ ]   [ ]   [ ]

3 marks

Challenge 2

1. Count the objects and write the totals.

a) [ ] satsumas

b) [ ] apples

2. Continue the number sequence, counting in steps of 5.

0   5   [ ]   [ ]   [ ]   [ ]

3 marks

Challenge 3

1. Count the objects and write the totals.

a) [ ] pencils

b) [ ] pencils

2. Continue the number sequence, counting in steps of 10.

0   10   [ ]   [ ]   [ ]   [ ]

3 marks

Total: [ ] / 9 marks

Had a go [ ]   Getting there [ ]   Got it! [ ]

More, less and equals

- Work with numbers using a number line
- Use the terms *equals*, *more than* and *less than*

Equals

Equals means 'the same as'.

Example

> 4 is the same as 4. They are equal.

This scale is balanced because there are 4 marbles on each side. 4 is the same as 4.

4 equals 4, 4 = 4

More and less

More means a bigger total. A number that is bigger has a higher value. This is **more**.

Less means a smaller total. A number that is smaller has a lower value. This is **less**.

Example

There are 6 marbles on one side and 5 marbles on the other side. 6 is more than 5. This can be seen on a number line and on a balance scale.

> 6 is more than 5

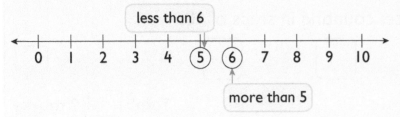

> less than 6

> more than 5

The balance scale tips to the side holding 6 marbles because 6 is more than 5. 6 has a higher value than 5.

Remember

Adding to a number will make the number bigger or **more** than it was before. Taking away from a number will make the number smaller or **less** than it was before.

Tip

Try making some towers of cubes with different heights. The biggest tower has the most cubes. The smallest tower has the least cubes.

Key word

- equals

Challenge 1

1. Look at the amounts. Tick the box for the amount that has more.

a) ☐ ☐

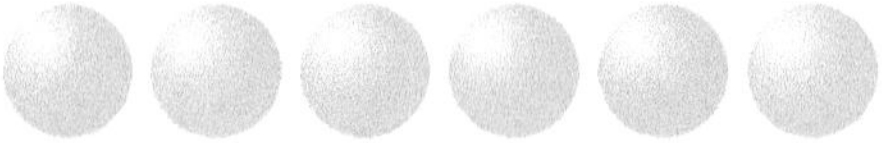

b) ☐ ☐

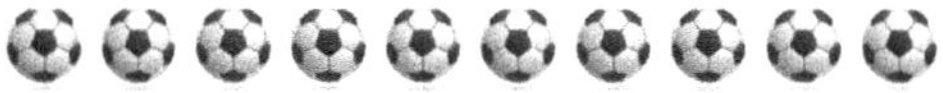

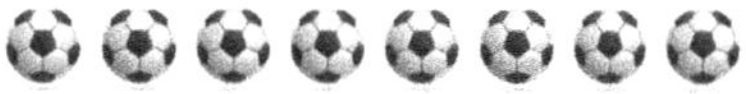

c) ☐ ☐

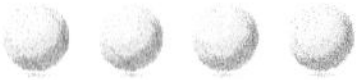

3 marks

Challenge 2

1. Look at the balance scales. Complete the sentences by writing the amounts that are in each side.

a)

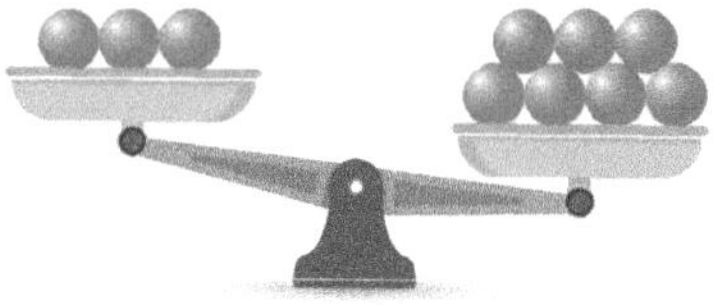

☐ is less than ☐

b)

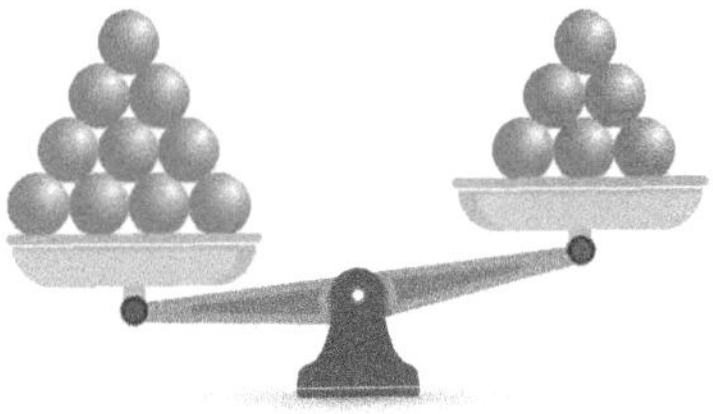

☐ is more than ☐

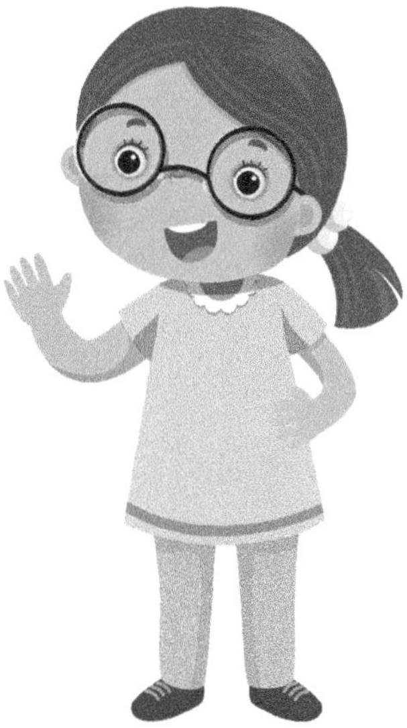

2 marks

Challenge 3

1. Complete the sentences by writing **more** or **less**.

a) 8 is ____________ than 9

b) 11 is ____________ than 12

c) 18 is ____________ than 15

d) 13 is ____________ than 19

4 marks

Total: ☐ / 9 marks

Had a go ☐ Getting there ☐ Got it! ☐

Number bonds and facts to 10

- Know number bonds and subtraction facts from 0 to 10
- Solve one-step problems for addition and subtraction

Number facts and bonds

A **number fact** (or **bond**) is a **pair** of numbers that **equal** an amount. Different pairs of numbers can equal the same amount.

Example

There are six possible ways to make 5. These are the number facts to 5:

0 + 5

1 + 4

2 + 3

3 + 2

4 + 1

5 + 0

Here is a **fact family** for one fact for the number 5:

1 + 4 = 5 and **4 + 1 = 5**   **5 − 1 = 4** and **5 − 4 = 1**

There are two additions and two subtractions.

Example

There are lots of ways to make 10. These are the number facts to 10:

0 + 10   1 + 9   2 + 8   3 + 7   4 + 6   5 + 5

6 + 4   7 + 3   8 + 2   9 + 1   10 + 0

Here is a fact family for one fact for the number 10:

1 + 9 = 10 and **9 + 1 = 10**   **10 − 1 = 9** and **10 − 9 = 1**

There are two additions and two subtractions.

Tip

Try using your fingers and thumbs to count facts to 5 and facts to 10.

Remember

There are normally two addition and two subtraction facts that go together. For example, 2 + 3 = 5, 3 + 2 = 5 and 5 − 3 = 2, 5 − 2 = 3. These are known as a 'fact family'.

Key words

- number fact
- number bond

Challenge 1

1. Look at the beads and complete the number sentences.

a)

$\boxed{} + \boxed{} = 5$

b)

$\boxed{} + \boxed{} = 5$

c)

$\boxed{} + \boxed{} = 10$

$\boxed{}$
3 marks

Challenge 2

1. Complete the number sentences.

a) $1 + \boxed{} = 5$ $\boxed{} + 0 = 5$ $2 + \boxed{} = 5$ $3 + \boxed{} = 5$

b) $10 - \boxed{} = 3$ $10 - \boxed{} = 1$ $10 - \boxed{} = 4$ $10 - \boxed{} = 2$

$\boxed{}$
8 marks

Challenge 3

1. Write **+** or **–** to complete the number sentences.

a) $1 \boxed{} 4 = 5$ $5 \boxed{} 4 = 1$ $3 \boxed{} 2 = 5$

b) $5 \boxed{} 5 = 10$ $10 \boxed{} 2 = 8$ $10 \boxed{} 5 = 5$

c) $1 \boxed{} 9 = 10$ $3 \boxed{} 7 = 10$ $10 \boxed{} 4 = 6$

$\boxed{}$
9 marks

Total: $\boxed{}$ / 20 marks

Had a go $\boxed{}$ Getting there $\boxed{}$ Got it! $\boxed{}$

Number bonds and facts to 20

- Know number bonds and subtraction facts from 0 to 20
- Solve one-step problems for addition and subtraction

Number facts and bonds up to 20

A **number fact** (or **bond**) is a pair of numbers that equal an amount. Lots of different pairs of numbers can equal the same amount. It is useful to know as many as you can.

Example

There are lots of ways to make 20. These are the number facts to 20.

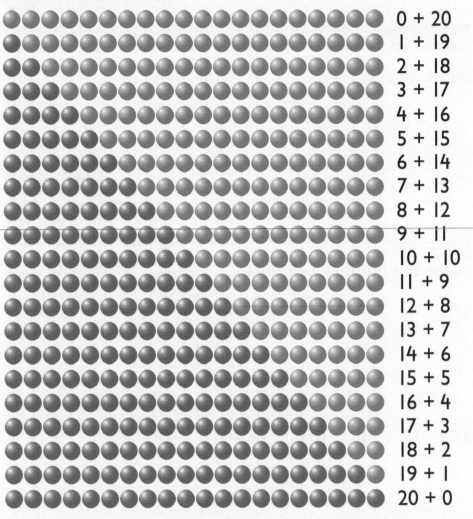

0 + 20
1 + 19
2 + 18
3 + 17
4 + 16
5 + 15
6 + 14
7 + 13
8 + 12
9 + 11
10 + 10
11 + 9
12 + 8
13 + 7
14 + 6
15 + 5
16 + 4
17 + 3
18 + 2
19 + 1
20 + 0

Here is a fact family for one fact for the number 20:

1 + 19 = 20 and 19 + 1 = 20
20 − 1 = 19 and 20 − 19 = 1

There are two additions and two subtractions.

Remember

Knowing facts to 20 is very useful for beginning to add a single-digit number to a two-digit number.

Tip

When you are confident you know number bonds to 10, take one fact, add 10 to one of the numbers, and you can instantly make a fact to 20. For example, 7 + 3 = 10, so 17 + 3 = 20.

Key words

- number fact
- number bond

Challenge 1

1. Look at the beads and complete the number sentences.

   a)

   [ ] + [ ] = 20

   b)

   [ ] + [ ] = 20

   c)

   [ ] + [ ] = 20

   d)

   [ ] + [ ] = 20

   [ ]
   4 marks

Challenge 2

1. Complete the number sentences.

   a) 1 + [ ] = 20   [ ] + 0 = 20   2 + [ ] = 20

   b) 20 − [ ] = 13   20 − [ ] = 17   20 − [ ] = 14

   [ ]
   6 marks

Challenge 3

1. Write **+** or **−** to complete the number sentences.

   a) 1 [ ] 19 = 20   20 [ ] 4 = 16   13 [ ] 7 = 20

   20 [ ] 15 = 5   12 [ ] 8 = 20

   b) 11 [ ] 9 = 20   18 [ ] 2 = 20   10 [ ] 10 = 20

   20 [ ] 19 = 1   3 [ ] 17 = 20

   [ ]
   10 marks

   Total: [ ] /20 marks

   Had a go [ ]   **Getting there** [ ]   **Got it!** [ ]

Adding and subtracting numbers to 20

- Add and subtract one-digit and two-digit numbers to 20
- Solve one-step problems that involve addition and subtraction

Adding a two-digit number and ones

To **add** a one-digit number (unit) to a two-digit number, start with the larger number and count on with the smaller number.

Example

11 + 5

Start at 11 on the **number line** and count on 5 jumps.

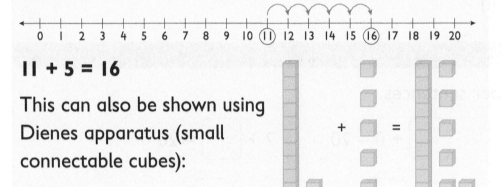

11 + 5 = 16

This can also be shown using Dienes apparatus (small connectable cubes):

Subtracting a one-digit number from a two-digit number

To **subtract** a one-digit number (unit) from a two-digit number, start with the larger number and count backwards with the smaller number.

Example

18 – 7

Start at 18 on the number line and count back 7 jumps.

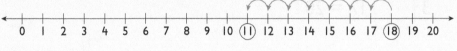

18 – 7 = 11

Key words

- addition
- number line
- subtraction

Challenge 1

1. Use the cubes to help you add the amounts. Write the answer in the box.

a) $10 + 6 = \boxed{}$

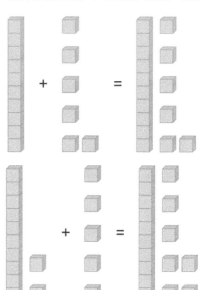

b) $12 + 5 = \boxed{}$

2 marks

Challenge 2

1. Use the number lines on the opposite page to help you add and subtract the numbers.

a) $11 + 9 = \boxed{}$ $14 + 4 = \boxed{}$

b) $19 - 9 = \boxed{}$ $17 - 5 = \boxed{}$

4 marks

Challenge 3

1. Complete the bar models by filling in the numbers. The top bar is the total. The two bars underneath make that total. One has been done for you.

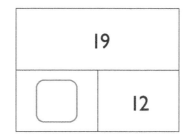

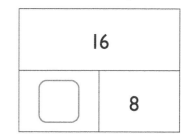

15
6   9

19
☐   12

16
☐   8

2. Complete the number sentences.

$9 = \boxed{} - 7$ $16 = \boxed{} - 3$ $7 = \boxed{} - 4$

$14 = \boxed{} - 6$ $14 = \boxed{} - 5$

7 marks

Total: $\boxed{}$ /13 marks

Had a go ☐   **Getting there** ☐   **Got it!** ☐

Multiples of 2, 5 and 10 with arrays

- Solve one-step problems for multiplication using arrays

Multiplication

Multiplication means lots of, or 'times by'.
Multiplication is **repeated addition** – it is like adding the same number lots of times.

Multiplication is an **operation**. It is shown by the symbol **x**.

Objects that are arranged in rows and columns to represent a multiplication are called an **array**.

Example

This array shows the multiplication 4 x 2
When you count the circles in each column, two are added each time in this order: 2, 4, 6, 8
There are 8 circles in total (4 x 2 = 8).

> There are four columns, with two circles in each column.

This array shows the multiplication 3 x 5
When you count the circles in each column, five are added each time in this order: 5, 10, 15
There are 15 circles in total (3 x 5 = 15).

> There are three columns, with five circles in each column.

This array shows the multiplication 2 x 10
When you count the circles in each column, ten are added each time in this order: 10, 20
There are 20 circles in total (2 x 10 = 20).

> There are two columns, with ten circles in each column.

Key words

- multiplication
- repeated addition
- operation
- array

1. Look at the arrays and complete the number sentences.

a)

b)

2 + 2 + 2 + 2 + 2 = ☐

5 + 5 + 5 + 5 + 5 = ☐

2 marks

2. Complete each calculation and match it to the correct array.

10 x 5 = ☐

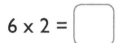

6 x 2 = ☐

2 marks

Challenge 2

Complete the sentence for each array.

1. a)

☐ columns of ☐ = ☐

b)

☐ columns of ☐ = ☐

2 marks

Challenge 3

1. Complete the table. The first row has been done for you.

Array	Repeated addition	Multiplication
4 columns of 2	2 + 2 + 2 + 2 = 8	4 x 2 = 8
2 columns of 2		2 x 2 = 4
	5 + 5 + 5 = 15	3 x 5 = 15
6 columns of 5	5 + 5 + 5 + 5 + 5 + 5 = 30	
2 columns of 10		2 x 10 = 20
5 columns of 10	10 + 10 + 10 + 10 + 10 = 50	

5 marks

Total: ☐ /11 marks

Had a go ☐   Getting there ☐   Got it! ☐

Sharing and grouping

- Understand sharing and grouping
- Solve one-step problems for division

Division

Division means to **share** into equal amounts or split into groups of the same amount. Division is an **operation**. It is shown by the symbol ÷.

When you **divide**, you divide the largest number.

Sharing

When you divide by **sharing**, a larger number is shared out equally between groups so that each smaller amount is the same. This is **sharing equally between**.

Example

If eight marbles are shared equally into two piles, each pile has four marbles.

 shared by 2 =

The **calculation** is 8 ÷ 2 = 4

Grouping

When you divide by **grouping**, a larger number is split to find how many groups there can be with the same amount in each. This is **grouping into equal sets**.

Example

If eight marbles are grouped into twos, it means that four equal sets are made.

 in groups of 2 =

> **Remember**
>
> **Odd numbers** such as 1, 3, 5 and 7 cannot be divided equally into whole numbers.

> **Remember**
>
> Always divide the largest number by the smaller number.

> **Tip**
>
> Gather objects and share them out between people. Divide an **even number** of objects into groups of two and then count the number of groups.

> **Key words**
>
> - division
> - sharing
> - operation
> - odd numbers
> - calculation
> - grouping
> - even numbers

Challenge 1

1. Share 6 marbles between two.
   Draw the marbles in the circles.

2. Complete the sentences. Write the answers in the boxes.

There are ☐ marbles altogether. There are ☐ groups. There are

☐ marbles in each group.

2 marks

Challenge 2

1. Draw lines to match the sentences to the pictures.

12 shared by 2 = 6

12 shared by 4 = 3

12 shared by 3 = 4

3 marks

Challenge 3

1. Look at the array. Complete the table.

Sharing and grouping	Calculation
6 groups of 3	6 x 3
3 groups of 6	☐ x 6
18 shared by ☐	18 ÷ 6
18 shared by 3	18 ÷ ☐
18 in groups of 6	18 ÷ 6
18 in groups of ☐	18 ÷ 3

4 marks

Total: ☐ /9 marks

Had a go ☐   **Getting there** ☐   **Got it!** ☐

Doubling and halving

- Solve one-step problems for multiplication and division
- Double and halve numbers

Doubling

When you **multiply** any number by 2, you **double** its value. This means there are twice as many.

Doubling can be shown by writing **x 2** (multiply by 2). Adding the same number twice is also doubling. Any number can be doubled.

Example

Here are 4 crayons.

If you multiply the number of crayons by 2, you add another 4 crayons. Now the number of crayons has been doubled so there are 8.

Double 4 is 8 or 4 + 4 = 8 or 4 x 2 = 8

Halving

When you **divide** any number by 2, you **halve** its value. This means there is only half as much.

Halving can be shown by writing ÷ **2** (divide or share by 2).

Odd numbers ending in 1, 3, 5, 7 and 9 cannot be divided in half equally.

Example

Here are 8 crayons.

If you divide the number of crayons by 2, you halve the number of crayons. This leaves 4.

Half of 8 is 4 or 8 – 4 = 4 or 8 ÷ 2 = 4

Remember

Halving is the inverse (opposite) of doubling, and doubling is the inverse of halving.

Tip

When a number is halved, multiply that number by 2 to get back to the original number.
When a number is doubled, divide that number by 2 to get back to the original number.

Key words

- multiplication
- division

Challenge 1

1. Double the objects that you can see by drawing the same number of objects in the box. Then write the total.

= ☐

2. Halve the objects that you can see by crossing out half of them. Then write the total left in the box.

 = ☐

☐ 2 marks

Challenge 2

1. The spots in the arrays are in two colours. Complete the number sentence to show the double.

a) 2 × ☐ = ☐

b) 2 × ☐ = ☐

☐ 4 marks

Challenge 3

1. Complete the bar models by filling in the numbers. The top is the total. The two boxes underneath make that total.

a) Double the number to find the total.

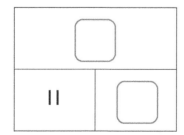

☐	
11	☐

b) Halve the total equally to find the missing parts.

24	
☐	☐

☐ 4 marks

Total: ☐ /10 marks

Had a go ☐   **Getting there** ☐   **Got it!** ☐

Progress test 2

1. Look at the measuring tapes and fill in the missing numbers.

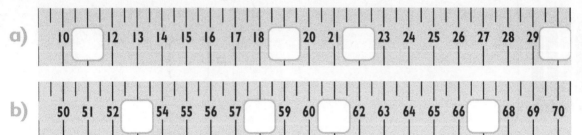

a) 10 ☐ 12 13 14 15 16 17 18 ☐ 20 21 ☐ 23 24 25 26 27 28 29 ☐

b) 50 51 52 ☐ 54 55 56 57 ☐ 59 60 ☐ 62 63 64 65 66 ☐ 68 69 70

2 marks

2. Complete the calculations.

a) 5 + 0 = ☐

b) 3 + 7 = ☐

c) 5 − 3 = ☐

3 marks

3. Look at the number square. Write in the missing numbers.

1		3		5		7		9	
11		13		15		17		19	
21		23		25		27		29	
31		33		35		37		39	

1 mark

4. Complete the table. Write one more and one less of each number.

One less	Number	One more
	6	
	17	
	44	
	59	
	87	
	101	

12 marks

5. A toy shop is having a sale. All the items are half price. Find the new price of each item.

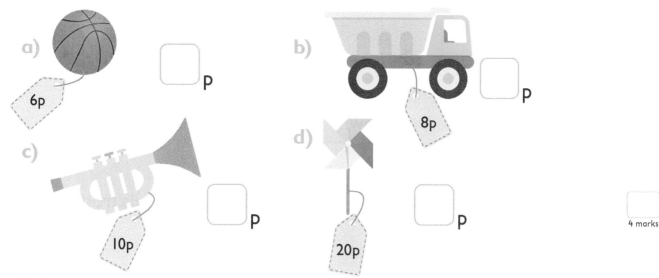

a) ☐ p

6p

b) ☐ p

8p

c) ☐ p

10p

d) ☐ p

20p

4 marks

6. Write these numbers as words.

1 _____   5 _____   14 _____

3 marks

7. Alice and James are skipping.

a) Alice skips for 10 seconds. She does 11 skips. She then skips for 10 more seconds and she does 9 skips. How many skips does she do altogether? ☐

b) James skips for 10 seconds. He does 10 skips. He skips again and adds his skips to the 10 he did before. He counts 19 in total. How many skips does he do the second time? ☐

2 marks

8. Use the marbles to help calculate the answers.

a) 2 + 3 = ☐ ●● ●●●

b) 4 + 1 = ☐ ●●●● ●

2 marks

9. Jessica has 10 apples. Tom has three fewer apples than Jessica. How many apples does Tom have? ☐

1 mark

10. Complete the calculations.

a) $12 + 8 =$ ☐   ☐ $= 11 + 9$ $20 =$ ☐ $+ 13$

b) $20 - 14 =$ ☐ $20 - 18 =$ ☐ $15 = 20 -$ ☐   ☐ 6 marks

PS 11. a) Yusuf has 20 satsumas but gives 8 to his friend Eva.
How many does he have now?

☐

b) Yusuf collects 11 shells at the beach. Eva collects 9 shells from the beach.
How many shells do they have in total?

☐   ☐ 2 marks

12. Use the number line to help you calculate the answers.

0 1 2 3 4 5 6 7 8 9 10 11 12 13 14 15 16 17 18 19 20

a) $14 + 5 =$ ☐   b) $17 - 9 =$ ☐   c) $6 + 14 =$ ☐   ☐ 3 marks

PS 13. There are 5 shelves in the toy shop. Each shelf has 5 teddy bears.

How many teddy bears are on the shelves altogether?   ☐   ☐ 1 mark

PS 14. A bouncy ball costs 10p. James buys 5 bouncy balls.

How much does he spend in total?

☐   ☐ 1 mark

PS 15. Ding buys two toy trains. He spends 20p.

How much does **one** toy train cost?

☐   ☐ 1 mark

16. Some children have some sweets.

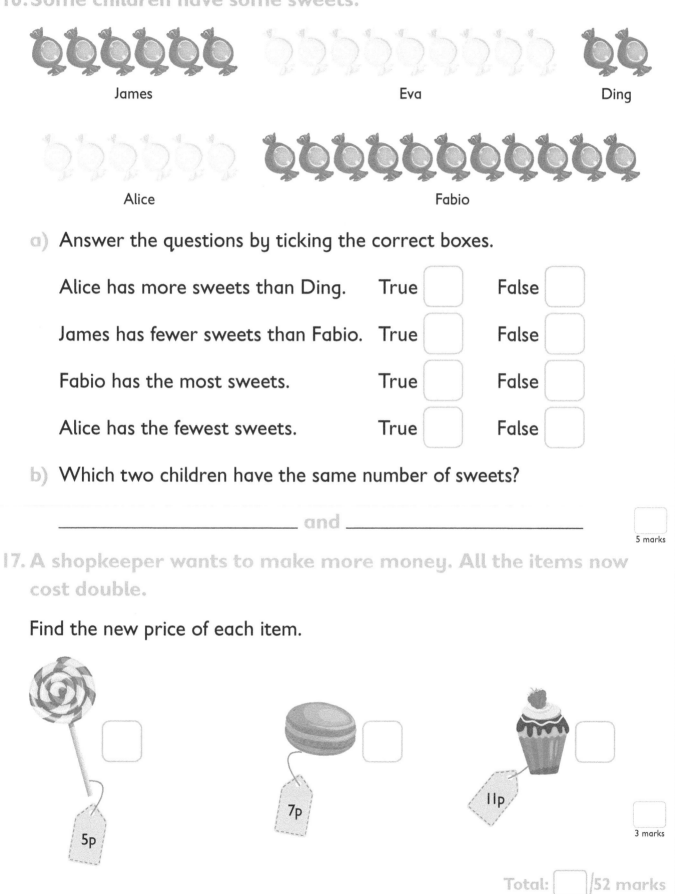

James

Eva

Ding

Alice

Fabio

a) Answer the questions by ticking the correct boxes.

Alice has more sweets than Ding.   True ☐   False ☐

James has fewer sweets than Fabio.   True ☐   False ☐

Fabio has the most sweets.   True ☐   False ☐

Alice has the fewest sweets.   True ☐   False ☐

b) Which two children have the same number of sweets?

_____ and _____   ☐

5 marks

17. A shopkeeper wants to make more money. All the items now cost double.

Find the new price of each item.

☐   5p

☐   7p

☐   11p

3 marks

Total: ☐ /52 marks

49

Handwriting

- Recognise letters of the alphabet
- Form lower-case letters in the correct direction, starting and finishing in the right place

Capital and lower-case letters

The letters of the alphabet all have a **capital letter** (**upper-case**) form and a **lower-case** letter form.

abcdefghijklmnopqrstuvwxyz

ABCDEFGHIJKLMNOPQRSTUVWXYZ

The letters below are all very similar in size. These are **lower-case** letters. When writing the letters, start at the red dot, and follow the arrow to form the letter.

Letters with descenders and ascenders

Some letters have **descenders** or **ascenders**. These are parts of the letter that go below or above other letters.

The letters below show the correct length of descenders and ascenders.

part of the letter is below the line – these are descenders

part of the letter is above the line – these are ascenders

Key words

- capital letter
- upper-case
- lower-case
- descenders
- ascenders

1. Trace each of the letters, then write each one again. Keep the letters a consistent size.

a   e   i

o   u

5 marks

1. Trace each of these letters, then write each one again. Keep the ascenders and descenders a consistent size.

b   d   h

g   p   y

6 marks

1. Copy the words carefully, thinking about how each letter should be formed.

a) a black cat

_____

b) a long river

_____

2 marks

Total: ☐ /13 marks

Had a go ☐   **Getting there** ☐   **Got it!** ☐

The alphabet and sounds

- Recognise letters of the alphabet
- Distinguish between alternative spellings of the same sound

Letters and sounds

Each letter of the alphabet has at least one sound.

Example

'a' can make a short sound as in c**a**t,
or a long sound as in c**a**ke.
'e' can make a short sound as in b**e**d,
or a long sound as in th**e**se.

Words with **vowel** sounds are sometimes spelled using different letters to make that sound.

Example

short **e** sound – **ea** as in h**ea**d
short **i** sound – **y** as in g**y**m
short **o** sound – **a** as in w**a**tch

> The vowel sounds in these words are made using different letters.

Each spelling pattern below makes the long vowel sound like its letter name.

a	e	i	o	u
a – e made	**e – e** these	**i – e** five	**o – e** home	**u – e** June
ai rain	**ee** see	**ie** lie	**oa** boat	**oo** food
ay day	**ea** sea	**igh** night	**oe** toe	**ue** blue
A April	**ie** chief	**y** cry	**ow** own	**ew** new
	ey key			**ou** you

Remember

The 'magic e' at the end of a word makes the previous vowel say its name, not its sound, e.g. f**a**t, f**a**te; b**i**t, b**i**te, n**o**t, n**o**te; c**u**t, c**u**te.

Key words

- capital letter
- upper-case
- lower-case
- vowel

Challenge 1

1. Match each lower-case letter to its capital. The first one has been done for you.

a   b   d   e   g   h   i   l   n   q   r   t   y

E   H   Y   A   T   B   G   I   R   L   Q   N   D

☐ 12 marks

Challenge 2

1. Add the correct letters to complete each spelling.

h __ v __   sp __ d__   f__ v __   b __ n __

   5   

☐ 4 marks

Challenge 3

1. Copy and complete each sentence with the correct spelling. Then write the letter name for the vowel sound already given.
The first one has been done for you.

a) My _h_ o _m_ e is where I live.   __o__

b) The __ ai __ poured down.   _____

c) They saw a big __oa__ on the water.   _____

d) The stars can be seen at __ igh __.   _____

e) Last night I had a __ rea __
that I went to space.   _____

☐ 4 marks

Total: ☐ /20 marks

Had a go ☐   **Getting there** ☐   **Got it!** ☐

Tricky words

- Spell common exception words
- Spell the days of the week

Exception words

Exception words are words that do not follow a **spelling rule**. Even if the word is segmented into syllables and sounds, it can still be tricky to spell.

Example

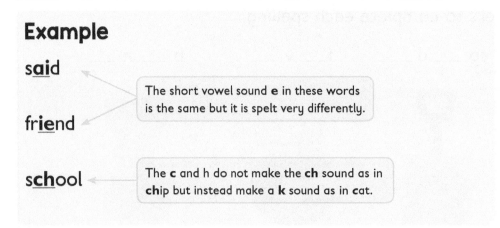

s<u>ai</u>d

fri<u>e</u>nd

> The short vowel sound **e** in these words is the same but it is spelt very differently.

s<u>ch</u>ool

> The **c** and h do not make the **ch** sound as in **ch**ip but instead make a **k** sound as in **c**at.

Take care when spelling the underlined sounds in the following examples:

<u>o</u>ne   s<u>o</u>me   on<u>c</u>e   s<u>ay</u>s

Days of the week

'Wednesday' is the trickiest day of the week to spell because, for most people, the **d** is silent. But it should be learned just like the other days of the week. Try breaking the word down and saying the 'd' out loud to remind you: Wed-nes-day.

Monday	Tuesday	Wednesday
Thursday	Friday	Saturday	Sunday

Make sure you always use a **capital letter** at the beginning of each day of the week.

Challenge 1

1. Read each word below. Then cover it up and try to write it correctly on the line below.

no   his   has   says   one

_____   _____   _____   _____   _____

5 marks

Challenge 2

1. Read each day of the week. Then cover it up and try to write it correctly on the line below.

Monday   Tuesday   Wednesday

_____   _____   _____

Thursday   Friday   Saturday

_____   _____   _____

Sunday

_____

7 marks

Challenge 3

1. Choose the correct word to complete each sentence below. Then cover it up and try to write the word correctly on the line.

friend   **said**   **Once**

a) _____ upon a time, there was a pink elephant.

b) "It is time for tea," _____ Dad.

c) My _____ is called Sam.

3 marks

Total: [   ] /15 marks

Had a go [ ]   **Getting there** [ ]   **Got it!** [ ]

Prefixes and suffixes

- Spell words with the prefix *un-* added
- Know and use the spelling rule for adding *-s* and *-es* to words

Adding the prefix un-

Adding the **prefix** **un-** to the start of a word gives the word the opposite meaning.

Example

happy ⟶ **un-** + happy = **un**happy

lock ⟶ **un-** + lock = **un**lock

tie ⟶ **un-** + tie = **un**tie

Remember

To spell words with un-, simply write 'un' at the start of the word.

Adding the suffix -s or -es

Adding the **suffix** **-s** or **-es** changes a word from **singular** to **plural**.

Using **-s** or **-es** depends on the original ending of the **root word**.

Tip

Try to remember spelling rules.

Most plural words are spelt by adding **-s** to the word. But, if the word ends in x, z, s, ch or sh, then **-es** is added.

Example

gate → gate**s**   car → car**s**   rabbit → rabbit**s**

box → box**es**   bus → bus**es**   chur**ch** → chur**ches**

These rules also apply if you are spelling an action word (**verb**) that shows what somebody is doing.

Example

she run**s**   he swim**s**   it jump**s**

she miss**es**   it buzz**es**   it smash**es**

Key words

- prefix
- suffix
- singular
- plural
- root word
- verb

Challenge 1

1. Discuss with a grown-up what each word means and then add **un-** to give the opposite meaning.

___kind   ___safe   ___tidy   ___true   ___helpful

5 marks

Challenge 2

1. Look at the ending of each of these words. Decide whether each word should have **-s** or **-es** added to make it plural. Write the plural word underneath.

tree   hat   brush   apple

_____   _____   _____   _____

bunch   house   bus   boat

_____   _____   _____   _____

8 marks

Challenge 3

1. Re-write the underlined verb from each sentence with the correct ending.

a) She <u>run</u> a race. _____

b) He <u>wash</u> his hands. _____

c) The wind <u>blow</u> the trees. _____

d) She <u>smash</u> the plate. _____

e) The light <u>flash</u> in the dark. _____

f) Ben <u>eat</u> his lunch. _____

g) Daisy <u>jump</u> over the fence. _____

h) Tom <u>munch</u> his burger. _____

8 marks

Total: ☐ /21 marks

Had a go ☐   **Getting there** ☐   **Got it!** ☐

More suffixes

- Add *-ing, -ed, -er* and *-est* to words when no change is needed to the root word

Adding a suffix

In many cases, a **suffix** can be added to a word without changing the **root word**.

Adding the suffixes **-ing**, **-er** and **-est** mean the root word stays the same. Adding these suffixes always adds an extra syllable to a word. The suffix **-ed** sometimes adds an extra syllable to a word.

Remember

Adding **-er** to an action word (verb) changes the word to a naming word (**noun**).

Example

Action words (verbs)

jump
Kate can jump. ⇨ Kate is jump**ing**. ⇨ Kate jump**ed**. ⇨ Kate is a jump**er**.

> Adding -er makes a naming word (noun) – 'jumper'

paint
I paint pictures. ⇨ I am paint**ing** pictures. ⇨ I paint**ed** pictures. ⇨ I am a paint**er**.

> Adding -er makes a naming word (noun) – 'painter'

The suffixes **-er** and **-est** are added to describing words. The root word doesn't change but adding these suffixes adds an extra syllable.

Remember

Describing words such as 'great' do not have **-ing** endings.

Example

Describing words (adjectives)

great
Al is great. ⇨ Al is the great**est**. ⇨ Al is great**er**.

quick
Jo is quick. ⇨ Jo is the quick**est**. ⇨ Jo is quick**er** than Ali.

Key words

- suffix
- root word
- verb
- noun
- adjective

Challenge 1

1. Remove the ending in each word below and write the root word.

   a) helping _____

   b) rower _____

   c) building _____

   d) looked _____

   e) walked _____

   f) kicking _____

   6 marks

Challenge 2

1. Complete the words in each sentence with the correct ending.

   a) My dad is a cook. He is great at cook_____.

   b) Lou likes to eat. She is always eat_____.

   c) Zen walks to school. Yesterday he walk_____ home too.

   d) My tortoise came last in the pets' race. It was the slow_____ pet.

   4 marks

Challenge 3

1. Complete the passage below. Use the given root words and add the correct ending to each.

   eat   **wash**   **mix**   **help**

   Sam was _____ his hands. His mum was

   _____ ingredients for cupcakes.

   Sam _____ by _____ some of
   the cupcake mixture!

   4 marks

   Total: [   ]/14 marks

Had a go [   ]   **Getting there** [   ]   **Got it!** [   ]

Planning writing

- Say out loud what your piece of writing will be about

Ideas for writing

People write for all sorts of reasons. To begin with, you need to have an idea of what you want to write, for example:

- Re-tell a story you know, or write a new story.

- Write an information text about a hobby you enjoy.

- Write instructions on how to do something.

Tip

Write about something you know about. What do you like doing? What stories do you know?

Plans for writing

Ideas can be made into a **plan** of what the writing will say.

The plan for a story needs to include:

- Who is it about?

- What do they do?

- What happens in the story?

The plan for an information text or instructions needs to include:
- What are the main ideas or points?

- What do you want the reader to know?

Sharing ideas and plans

Talking about an idea with someone else can help you check if it makes sense.

Say ideas out loud and ask others what they think.

Think carefully about planning from an idea. Again, see what others think.

A plan will help you to keep key information in the right order. This is important for stories and instructions.

Tip

Talk about the main parts of your idea. You don't have to tell the whole story yet.

Key word

- plan

1. Share a story idea with a grown-up for each of these story titles. Describe what happens or could happen in the story. If you don't know the story, ask a grown-up to tell it to you.

Cinderella 	*Little Red Riding Hood* 	*Jack and the Beanstalk* 

3 marks

1. Share ideas about the sort of information you might find in texts with the following titles.

a) People who help us
b) Space
c) Pets

3 marks

1. Think of something you want to write about. Answer these questions about it.

What will you write about?

What are the main points or events?

What will you write about first?

What else will you include?

Is there anything else you want to add?

5 marks

Total: ☐ /11 marks

Had a go ☐　　　**Getting there** ☐　　　**Got it!** ☐

Composing sentences

- Say a sentence out loud before writing it
- Form simple sentences using a capital letter and a full stop

Making sentences

Ideas and plans for writing need to be turned into **sentences**.

Before you write a sentence, make sure it sounds correct when you say it out loud.

Example

A fiction story

- **Idea** – boy called Jack, poor

  Sentence – Once upon a time, there was a poor boy called Jack.

- **Idea** – next morning, beanstalk in garden

  Sentence – The next morning, a huge, green beanstalk stood in Jack's garden.

Example

An information text about cars

- **Ideas** – different shapes, different sizes, four wheels, engine

  Sentences – Cars are different shapes and sizes. Cars have four wheels and an engine.

Every sentence should begin with a **capital letter** and end with a **full stop** (see page 68).

> **Tip**
>
> Do not put too much information into a sentence. Use new sentences for different information.

> 'Once upon a time' is a great way to start a story.

> When forming sentences add describing words (**adjectives**) like **huge** and **green** to help with description.

> **Remember**
>
> A sentence should start with a capital letter and have a full stop at the end.

> These sentences are correctly formed with capital letters and full stops.

> **Key words**
>
> - sentence
> - adjective
> - capital letter
> - full stop

Challenge 1

1. Draw lines to match each writing idea to the appropriate sentence.

Idea	Sentence
fairytale	A bus can carry lots of people.
cooking food	The chef prepares meals in the kitchen.
transport	The prince was saved by the princess.

3 marks

Challenge 2

1. Say a sentence out loud for each of the ideas below:

a) **Idea:** space, rocket, moon

b) **Idea:** new school, Freya, new friends

2 marks

Challenge 3

1. Write a sentence for each of the pictures.

a)

_____

_____

_____

b)

_____

_____

_____

2 marks

Total: ___/7 marks

Had a go ☐   **Getting there** ☐   **Got it!** ☐

Narrative writing

- Sequence sentences to form short narratives

Writing a narrative

To create any type of writing, a series of **sentences** need to be put together. This is known as **narrative** writing. Sentences need to be in the correct order or **sequence** so that the writing makes sense.

Example

Each picture below has a sentence that helps to tell a story.

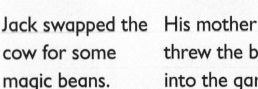

| Jack swapped the cow for some magic beans. | His mother threw the beans into the garden. | The next morning there was a huge beanstalk. |

Each sentence follows on from the previous sentence.

Example

The sentences below give instructions for growing a plant. The sentences have to be in the right order to make sense.

First put soil in a pot.

Next put the seeds into the soil.

Water the seeds every day.

See the plant grow.

Challenge 1

1. Read the sentences. Write **1, 2** and **3** in the boxes to put them in the correct order.

The next morning, he saw the huge beanstalk.

Carefully, Jack started to climb the beanstalk.

Jack's mother threw the beans into the garden.

3 marks

Challenge 2

1. Compose a sequence of sentences for the next part of the tale of *Jack and the Beanstalk* – the part where Jack gets to the top, sees the giant's castle, and the giant appears. Use the pictures to help you write sentences.

_____

_____

_____

_____

_____

_____

3 marks

Challenge 3

1. Tell a grown-up a sequence of three sentences for a part of a story you know.

3 marks

Total: ⬚ /9 marks

Had a go ⬚   **Getting there** ⬚   **Got it!** ⬚

Checking your writing

- Re-read writing to check that it makes sense

Making sure your writing is correct

It is important to read your writing to check that it makes sense. This is known as **proofreading**.

Whilst checking your writing, ask yourself these questions:

- Are the sentences in the correct order?

- Does each sentence make sense?

- Are words spelt correctly?

If you spot a mistake, cross it out neatly and correct your writing.

Remember

Always read what you have written to check that it makes sense.

Tip

Ask somebody else to read your writing too in case you miss any mistakes.

Example

Read the sentences below.

The princess went to the ball. ← Yes, this makes sense.

She had a lovely ← The sentence needs to be finished and a full stop added. Correct it by adding 'time' and a full stop.

She ran all the way home. ← This sentence is in the wrong place. It goes at the end. Correct it by crossing it out neatly and rewriting it at the end.

Soon it was time go. ← The word 'to' has been left out. Correct it by adding it in.

Key word

- proofread

Read this part of a well-known story and use it to answer the questions.

Little Red Riding Hood walked through
the forest.
She was going to visit her grandma.
The wolf followed her.
Once upon a time there was a girl called Little
Red Riding Hood.
Soon, she arrived at Grandma's house.

Challenge 1

1. Discuss the answers to these questions with a grown-up.

   a) Which sentence is in the wrong place?

   b) Where should it go?

   c) How do you know?

   3 marks

Challenge 2

1. Talk about how you can make these sentences better.

   a) The wolf followed her.

   > What was the wolf like? Add a word or two to describe it.

   b) Soon, she arrived at
   Grandma's house.

   > What was her grandma's house like? Add a word or two to describe it.

   2 marks

Challenge 3

1. Say or write sentences of your own that could be added after each of the following sentences from the passage.

   a) Little Red Riding Hood walked through the forest.

   As she walked, she _____

   b) Soon, she arrived at Grandma's house.

   Little Red Riding Hood _____

   2 marks

   Total: ____ /7 marks

Had a go ☐   Getting there ☐   Got it! ☐

Capital letters and full stops

- Punctuate sentences using a capital letter and a full stop
- Leave spaces between words when writing sentences

Using capital letters and full stops

Every sentence should begin with a **capital letter**.

The most common **punctuation** at the end of a sentence is a **full stop**.

Example

The fox is happy.

capital letter   full stop

Leaving spaces between words

Every single word in a sentence must have a space after it before you write the next word. Using your finger can help you to make sure you leave enough space.

Example

Read the text below, which has no capital letters or full stops, and some missing spaces.

the dog was hungryhe found a bone it was under thebush the bone was tasty the dog wagged histail he was happy

The text is difficult to read because it is not clear where words and sentences begin and end. It is also hard to decide which information is in each sentence.

Now read the text again, this time with the capital letters, full stops and spaces added:

The dog was hungry. He found a bone. It was under the bush. The bone was tasty. The dog wagged his tail. He was happy.

Challenge 1

1. Write each sentence again, making sure you use capital letters and full stops.

   a) my bike is fast _____

   _____

   b) the tree is tall _____

   _____

   c) it is a sunny day _____

   _____

   6 marks

Challenge 2

1. Read the sentences below. Circle each letter that should be a capital letter. Add in the missing full stops.

   a) we went to the shop mum got a new dress

   b) dad was making lunch he is a good cook

   8 marks

Challenge 3

1. Read the text and then write it again as five separate sentences with capital letters, full stops and correct spaces between words.

   it was a hot day   the dogwas hot   the girl was hot

   the girl jumped in thewater   the dog jumped inthe water

   _____

   _____

   _____

   _____

   13 marks

   Total: ☐ /27 marks

Had a go ☐   **Getting there** ☐   **Got it!** ☐

More capital letters

- Use a capital letter for names of people, places and days of the week
- Use a capital 'I' when using the personal pronoun 'I'

Capital letters for names

Capital letters are not only used at the beginning of **sentences**. They are also used for **names**, including names of **people**, names of **places** and names of **days** of the week.

Example

Names of people: This is **T**om.

Here is **J**ess.

Names of places: **T**om lives in **L**ondon.

London is in **G**reat **B**ritain.

Days of the week: **M**onday

Tuesday

Wednesday

Thursday

Friday

Saturday

Sunday

Using the personal pronoun 'I'

When writing 'I' in a sentence, a capital letter is always used, not the lower-case letter 'i'.

Example

Today **I** went to school. For lunch **I** ate fish. **I** liked it.

> **Remember**
>
> Capital letters for names can appear anywhere in a sentence.

> **Remember**
>
> If something is given a name, it needs a capital letter.

> **Key words**
>
> - capital letter
> - sentence

Challenge 1

1. Write each sentence again, making sure you use capital letters in the correct places.

    a) my name is fred. _____

    b) we are visiting sam. _____

    c) on sunday, they went swimming. _____

    _____

Challenge 2

1. Read the sentences below. Circle each letter that should be a capital letter.

    a) on friday, we went to wales.

    b) at school, i saw anna.

    c) leila went to london with jess.

Challenge 3

1. Re-write each pair of sentences with capital letters and correct punctuation.

    a) my friend jack has a big house. he lives in paris in france

    _____

    _____

    b) on mondays, i play the flute My teacher is called helen.

    _____

    _____

Total: ___ / 26 marks

Had a go ☐   **Getting there** ☐   **Got it!** ☐

Question marks

- Punctuate sentences using a question mark

Using a question mark

A **question mark** is a type of **punctuation** that can be used at the end of a **sentence**.

If the sentence is a **question**, a question mark is used instead of a full stop.

Example

Do you want to play?

What would you like for tea?

question mark

Question words

These words are question words. They are used to ask questions. If you begin a sentence with any of these words, you must end it with a question mark.

- **Who**

  Who wants to play football?

- **What**

  What time is the train?

- **Where**

  Where shall I put the bags?

- **When**

  When is it time for lunch?

- **Why**

  Why is it always raining?

- **How**

  How do you draw a house?

Challenge 1

1. Underline the question word and add a question mark at the end of each sentence.

a) What is your name

b) How old are you

c) Where do you live

d) When is your birthday

Challenge 2

1. Read the sentences below. Put a tick next to each sentence that uses the question mark correctly.

a) Why is Amir so happy? ☐

b) Kane ate his lunch? ☐

c) You are a great friend? ☐

d) How do you run so fast? ☐

e) When will it snow? ☐

f) Where are my keys? ☐

Challenge 3

1. Read each answer then write a suitable question that would give that answer.

Answer   **Question**

a) My name is Dan.   _____

b) It is 3 o'clock.   _____

c) My favourite fruit is mango. _____

d) I am from England.   _____

Total: ☐ / 16 marks

Had a go ☐   Getting there ☐   Got it! ☐

Exclamation marks

- Punctuate sentences using an exclamation mark

Using an exclamation mark

Exclamation marks are used to punctuate **exclamation sentences** or sentences that show surprise or excitement.

Exclamation sentences start with 'How' or 'What', contain an action word (**verb**) and have an exclamation mark at the end.

Example

What an amazing view we saw!

How beautiful the flowers smelled!

How tall the puppy had grown!

What an incredible necklace you are wearing!

exclamation mark

A sentence that ends with an exclamation mark generally shows more excitement or emotion than a sentence without.

Example

The eagle flew over Eden's head.

⇩

How close the eagle flew to Eden's head!

The pie that Milan cooked tasted good.

⇩

What an awesome, tasty pie Milan had cooked!

1. Add an exclamation mark to the end of each sentence.

a) What a fantastic sunset that was

b) How amazing your painting is

c) What brilliant trainers you are wearing

d) How incredible that cake tastes

4 marks

1. Read the sentences below. Put a tick next to each sentence that uses the exclamation mark correctly.

a) What time is dinner!

b) What brilliant swimming that was!

c) It is a school day!

d) What fast driving that is!

e) How long is the trip!

f) What great strength she showed!

3 marks

1. Complete each sentence with suitable words followed by an exclamation mark. One has been done for you.

What an awful day _____ it has been! _____

a) What an incredible view _____

b) How fantastic his cake _____

c) How high Abi's jump _____

d) What an amazing _____

4 marks

Total: ____ / II marks

Had a go ☐   **Getting there** ☐   **Got it!** ☐

Using 'and'

- Join words and sentences using 'and'

Joining information

The word '**and**' is a **joining word** used to join information.

It can join two items in a sentence.

Example

I had fish **and** chips for my tea.

The snow was cold **and** wet.

Using 'and' can also join ideas from different sentences.

Example

The cat liked to play. She also liked to chase mice.

⇩

The cat liked to play **and** chase mice.

It is Lena's birthday. She is having a party.

⇩

It is Lena's birthday **and** she is having a party.

Tom is good at maths. He knows all the answers.

⇩

Tom is good at maths **and** he knows all the answers.

Remember

Joining information with 'and' can make sentences a little longer and more interesting.

Tip

Stop sentences becoming too long by only joining two pieces of information with 'and'.

Key word

- joining word

Challenge 1

1. Read each sentence and write '**and**' in the space provided.

   a) Dev plays chess _____ he is best in his class.

   b) Flo's favourite flavour of crisps is cheese _____ onion.

   c) The hill is steep _____ it has lots of trees.

Challenge 2

1. Join the two sentences together with the word '**and**'. One has been done for you.

   Lizzie went to the show. It was fantastic.
   Lizzie went to the show and it was fantastic.

   a) Lucy has a dog. It is called Sandy.

   _____

   b) The shop is big. It sells most things.

   _____

   c) I am in Year 1. My teacher is Mr Jones.

   _____

Challenge 3

1. Add the word '**and**', then finish each sentence with your own ending.

   a) They saw the swimming pool _____

   _____

   b) I went to see my cousin _____

   _____

   c) Mum likes to bake cakes _____

   _____

   Total: ☐ 9 marks

Had a go ☐   **Getting there** ☐   **Got it!** ☐

Progress test 3

1. **Complete the names of the days of the week.**

   M_____day   T_____day   We_____

   Th_____   F_____day   Sat_____

   S_____

2. **Complete the underlined words in each sentence with the correct ending.**

   a) The man was fast but the horse was <u>fast</u>_____.

   b) My dog likes to play. He is always <u>play</u>_____.

   c) It was quiet in the garden but even <u>quiet</u>_____ inside.

   d) My mum can paint pictures. She is great at <u>paint</u>_____.

3. **Write a sentence for each of the pictures.**

   a) _____

   _____

   _____

   b) _____

   _____

   _____

4. Read this passage from a book called 'Driver Jane' and then answer the questions.

> Jane is a bus driver. She has a big, green bus. Her bus has fifty seats.
>
> Jane's bus takes children to school and then takes them home again.
>
> Jane always has a big smile. She likes meeting so many people.

a) Who is the text about? _____

b) What is the bus like? _____

c) Why does Jane like her job? _____

d) Which two places does the bus take children to?

_____ and _____

5 marks

5. Tick the fact box that works best with the passage in Question 4.

| Jane has a dog. ☐ | Jane has been a bus driver for 15 years. ☐ | Some children walk to school. ☐ |

☐

1 mark

6. Look at the pictures and read the sentences. Write 1, 2 and 3 in the boxes to put them in the correct order.

Cinderella lost the slipper. ☐

Cinderella married the prince. ☐

Cinderella went to the ball. ☐

3 marks

79

7. **Read the text below and then answer the question.**

> Jensen was at the zoo. He was bored. The lions were asleep. The hippo just stood there. The giraffe did nothing. Even the monkeys just hid in the trees.
>
> Then he smiled. The tiger was growling. It was fierce. He could see its teeth. It was eating a big piece of meat.

Why did Jensen smile? Tick one.

He was bored. ☐   He liked animals. ☐   The tiger was exciting. ☐

☐

1 mark

8. **Re-write each pair of sentences with capital letters and correct punctuation.**

a) it is sunny outside. we will play in the garden

_____

b) james goes to church every Sunday He loves it

_____

c) my friend rishi lives in india

_____

d) the dog is called toby. it belongs to sophie.

_____   ☐

14 marks

80

9. Write each sentence again, making sure you use capital letters and full stops.

a) the snow is cold   _____

b) it is a red ball   _____

c) my kite is green   _____

d) her sister is emma   _____

8 marks

10. Think of and share ideas for information you might include in information texts that have these titles:

a) **Food We Eat**

b) **The Seaside**

c) **On the Farm**

_____   _____   _____

_____   _____   _____

_____   _____   _____

_____   _____   _____

_____   _____   _____

_____   _____   _____

3 marks

Total: [ ] /48 marks

Finding a half

- Recognise and find one half

What is a fraction?

A **fraction** is a part of a whole object, group of objects, shape or number.

Half of an object or shape

Example

Here is an orange. This is the **whole**.

When the orange is cut in half, it is **divided** into two equal parts (or **halves**):

      This is how we write one half: $\frac{1}{2}$

Here is a blue **circle**. This is the whole.

When the circle is cut in half, it is divided into two equal parts (or halves):

Each half of the circle is a semi-circle.

Half of an amount or number

Example

Here are **six** bananas:

To split the six bananas in half, they are shared into two equal groups:

  shared by 2 = and

So, half ($\frac{1}{2}$) of 6 is 3. We can write this as **6 ÷ 2 = 3**

> **Remember**
>
> The bottom number of a fraction tells you how many equal parts there are altogether that make the whole.

> The number at the top tells you how many parts of the whole; the number at the bottom tells you how many parts make up the whole. So this means one of the two parts, or one half.

> **Key words**
>
> - fraction
> - division
> - circle

> There are 6 bananas altogether, shared into two groups. There are 3 in each group.

Challenge 1

1. Tick the shapes that have been divided in half.

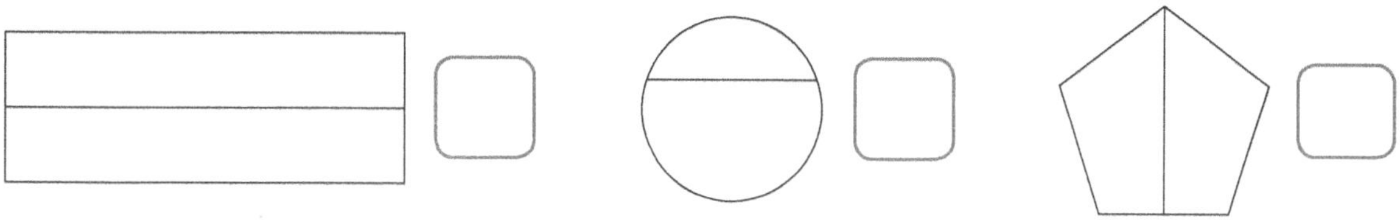

2 marks

2. Colour in half of each shape.

2 marks

Challenge 2

1. Draw a line through the middle of the shapes to split them in half. Use a ruler to help you.

3 marks

Challenge 3

1. Circle half of each group of objects.

2. Tick the amounts that have been divided in half.

a)

b)

c)

4 marks

Total: ☐ / 11 marks

Had a go ☐   Getting there ☐   Got it! ☐

Finding a quarter

- Recognise and find one quarter

Fractions

A **fraction** is a part of a whole object, group of objects, shape or number.

A quarter of an object or shape

Example

Here is an orange. This is the **whole**.

When the orange is cut into quarters, it is **divided** into four equal parts.

This is how we write one quarter: $\frac{1}{4}$

Here is a blue circle. This is the whole.

When the blue circle is cut into quarters, it is divided into four equal parts (or quarters).

Each part of the circle is one quarter, $\frac{1}{4}$

A quarter of an amount or number

Example

Here are eight tomatoes:

To split them into quarters, they are shared into four equal groups:

 shared by 4 =

So, one quarter $(\frac{1}{4})$ of 8 = 2. We can write the calculation as **8 ÷ 4 = 2**

Challenge 1

1. Tick the shapes that have been divided into quarters.

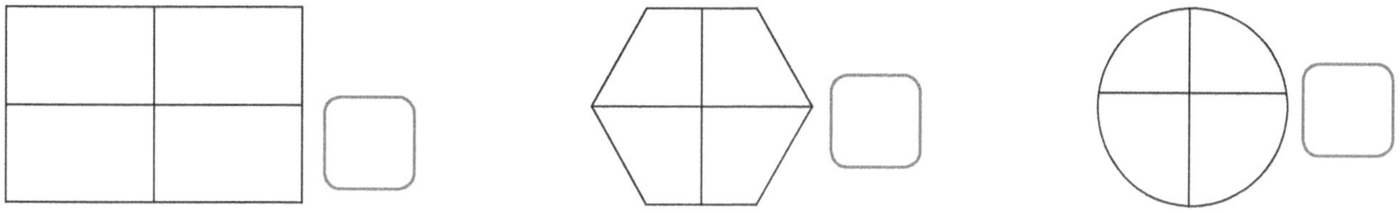

2 marks

2. Colour in a quarter of each shape.

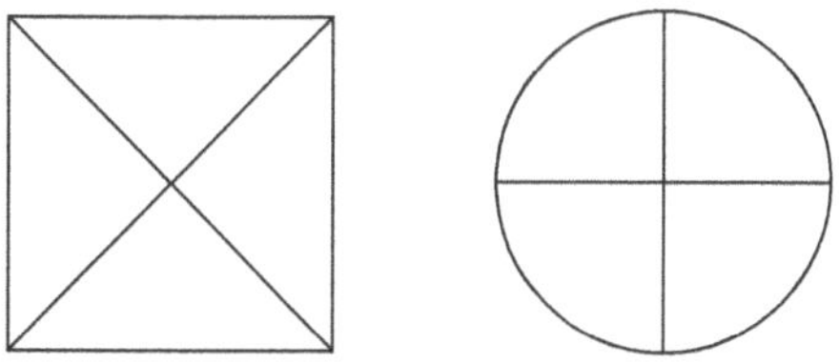

2 marks

Challenge 2

1. Draw two lines on the shapes to split them into quarters. Use a ruler to help you.

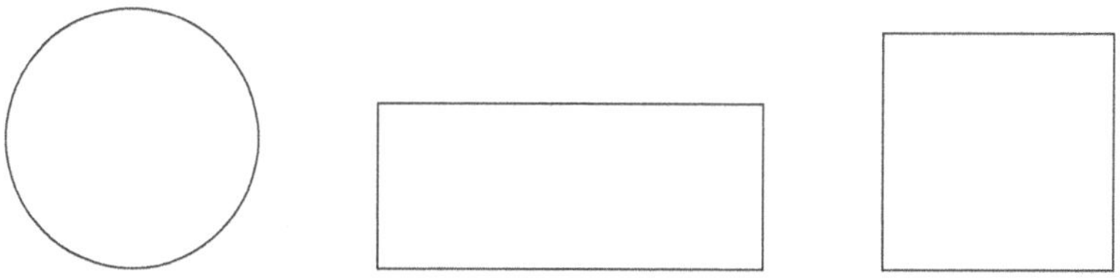

3 marks

Challenge 3

1. Circle a quarter of each group of objects.

2. Tick the amounts that have been divided into quarters.

a)

b)

c)

4 marks

Total: ☐ / 11 marks

Had a go ☐   Getting there ☐   Got it! ☐

85

Order of events

- Put events in the order in which they happen
- Know and use the words: day, week, month and year

Time

Time describes how long something takes to do, or how long something lasts.

- One **day** is 24 hours.
- One **week** is 7 days.
- One **month** is approximately 4 weeks.
- One **year** is 12 months.

Tip

Looking at a calendar every day is the best way to learn the days, weeks and months of the year.

Events in a day

Lots of things can happen in a day, so it is important to be able to put them in **order**.

Example

The first thing you do in a day is wake up, then you have breakfast. After that, you go to school. In the middle of the day, it is lunchtime. Then it is afternoon, followed by your evening meal. Finally, it is bedtime.

DAY

NIGHT

One full turn of the Earth = One full day

Days and months

There are 7 days in a week. The days fall in this order:

Monday	Tuesday	Wednesday	Thursday	Friday	Saturday	Sunday

There are 12 months in a year:

January is the first month and December is the last month. January is **earlier** in the year. December is **later** in the year.

Remember

Saturday and Sunday are known as the **weekend**.

Key word

- ordering

Challenge 1

1. If you need to, use the information on the opposite page to help you answer the questions.

   a) How many days are there in a week? ▢

   b) Approximately how many weeks are there in one month? ▢

   c) How many months are there in one year? ▢

   ▢ *3 marks*

Challenge 2

1. If you need to, use the days of the week list on the opposite page to help you answer the questions.

   a) Which day is after Tuesday? _____

   b) Which day is before Saturday? _____

   c) If yesterday was Monday and tomorrow is Wednesday, what day is it today?

   _____

   d) If tomorrow is Sunday, what day is it today? _____ ▢

   4 marks

Challenge 3

1. If you need to, use the months of the year cycle on the opposite page to help you answer the questions.

   a) What is the second month of the year? _____

   b) Which month is after March and before May? _____

   c) Which month is the second-to-last month of the year?

   _____

   d) What is the sixth month of the year? _____ ▢

   4 marks

   Total: ▢ / 11 marks

   Had a go ▢   **Getting there** ▢   **Got it!** ▢

Telling the time

- Tell the time to the hour and half past
- Draw the hands on a clock

What is time?

Time describes how long something takes to do, or how long something lasts.

Smaller amounts of time are measured in seconds, minutes and hours.

- There are 60 seconds in one minute.
- There are 60 minutes in one hour.
- There are 24 hours in one day.

A clock or watch is used to tell the time. There are two hands on a clock: the **hour hand** and the **minute hand**.

O'clock

When the minute hand is pointing to 12, it is showing a full hour. We call this time **o'clock**.

Example

The minute hand is pointing to the 12 and the hour hand is pointing to the 4. The clock is showing that the time is 4 o'clock.

Half past

When the minute hand is pointing to 6, it is showing half past the hour. We call this time **half past**.

Example

The minute hand is pointing to the 6 and the hour hand is pointing to halfway between 8 and 9. The clock is showing that the time is half past 8.

> **Remember**
>
> In 1 day there are 24 hours. In 1 hour there are 60 minutes. In 1 minute there are 60 seconds.

> This is the minute hand. It is longer than the hour hand.

> This is the hour hand. It is the shortest hand on the clock.

> **Tip**
>
> Think of half past as halfway around the clock.

Challenge 1

1. a) Tick the clock that shows 7 o'clock.

b) Tick the clock that shows half past 3.

2 marks

Challenge 2

1. Write the time the clocks show on the line. Here are some words to help.

one   two   three   four   five   six   seven   eight   nine   ten

eleven   twelve   o'clock   half past

_____   _____   _____   _____

_____   _____   _____   _____

4 marks

Challenge 3

1. Draw hands on the clocks to show the time.

2 o'clock   Half past 10   12 o'clock   Half past 9

4 marks

Total: ☐ /10 marks

Had a go ☐   **Getting there** ☐   **Got it!** ☐

Money

- Recognise and know the value of notes and coins

What is money?

Money is used to buy things. When paying for something at the shop, the items must be bought, or paid for, using money. Money comes in **coins** and **notes**.

In the UK, the standard units of money are **pounds** (£) and **pence** (p). Other countries use different units of money. Units of money are known as currency.

Each coin and note has a different value. The value of a coin or note is what it is worth.

Notes

Notes are worth more than coins.

The note shown above with the highest value is £20. It is worth 20 one-pound coins. The note with the lowest value is £5. It is worth 5 one-pound coins.

Coins

The coin with the highest value is £2. It is worth 200 pence. The coin with the lowest value is 1p.

The coins can be split up into pounds (£) and pence (p).

Remember

Notes and higher value coins mean you don't have to have lots and lots of 1p coins.

Tip

When using money, the value of the note or coin is always written on it.

Key word

- currency

Challenge 1

1. Look at the coins. Answer the questions.

a) How many 1p coins can you see? ☐

b) How many 10p coins can you see? ☐

c) How many £1 coins can you see? ☐

Challenge 2

1. Write the value of each coin.

a) ☐   b) ☐   c) ☐

d) ☐   e) ☐   f) ☐

Challenge 3

1. Look at the coins. Put them in order from least valuable to most valuable by writing the values in the boxes.

☐ ☐ ☐ ☐ ☐ ☐ ☐ ☐

least valuable   **most valuable**

Total: ☐ / 17 marks

Had a go ☐   Getting there ☐   Got it! ☐

2-D shapes

- Recognise and name 2-D shapes

What does 2-D mean?

2-D means **two dimensions**. 2-D shapes are **flat**.

Example

This is a square. It has two dimensions: the first dimension is up and down, and the second dimension is side to side.

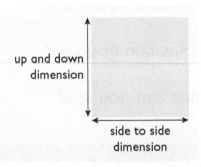

up and down dimension

side to side dimension

Here are the common 2-D shapes:

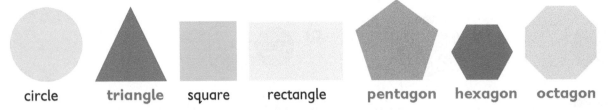

circle   triangle   square   rectangle   pentagon   hexagon   octagon

Here are some less common 2-D shapes:

semi-circle   oval   kite   heptagon   nonagon   decagon

Features of 2-D shapes

The features of 2-D shapes are called **properties**. They are the **sides** and the **vertices** (corners).

Example

A square has four sides and four corners. All the sides are the same length. All the sides are straight. All the corners are the same too.

Many everyday objects are based on 2-D shapes. They can be seen almost anywhere, for example, a clock, an oval-shaped mirror, a pizza, an envelope and road signs.

1. Draw a line to match each shape to its name.

rectangle   square   octagon   hexagon   circle   triangle   pentagon

1. For each of the shapes, fill in the boxes to show what properties they all have.

Number of sides [ ]   Number of corners [ ]

Number of sides [ ]   Number of corners [ ]

Number of sides [ ]   Number of corners [ ]

Number of sides [ ]   Number of corners [ ]

Number of sides [ ]   Number of corners [ ]

10 marks

1. Solve the riddle. What 2-D shape is it?

I have 4 sides.
I have 4 corners.
All my sides are the same.
What am I?

I am a _____

1 mark

Total: [ ] / 18 marks

Had a go [ ]   Getting there [ ]   Got it! [ ]

3-D shapes

- Recognise and name 3-D shapes

What does 3-D mean?

3-D means **three dimensions**. 3-D shapes are not flat – they are **solid**.

Example

This is a **cube**.
It has three dimensions.

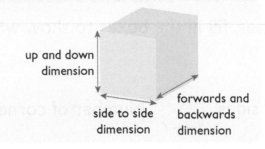

up and down dimension

side to side dimension

forwards and backwards dimension

Here are the common 3-D shapes:

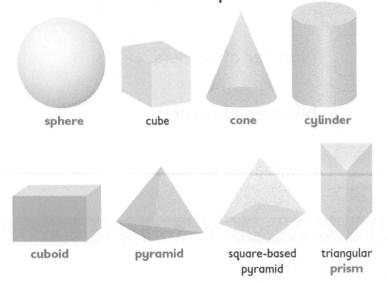

sphere   cube   cone   cylinder

cuboid   pyramid   square-based pyramid   triangular prism

Features of 3-D shapes

The features of 3-D shapes are called **properties**.
They are the **faces**, **edges**, and the **vertices** (corners).

Example

A cube has six square faces. All the faces are the same. All the edges are the same length. All the corners (vertices) are the same too.

Many everyday objects are based on 3-D shapes, for example, a cereal box, a teabag, a tin of soup and a tent.

Key words

- 3-D shape
- cube
- sphere
- cone
- cylinder
- cuboid
- pyramid
- prism
- face
- edge
- vertex/vertices

Challenge 1

1. Draw a line to match each shape to its name.

triangular prism   cube   cone   cylinder   cuboid   pyramid   sphere

7 marks

Challenge 2

1. For each of the shapes, fill in the boxes to show what properties they all have.

Number of faces ☐   Number of edges ☐   Number of vertices ☐

Number of faces ☐   Number of edges ☐   Number of vertices ☐

Number of faces ☐   Number of edges ☐   Number of vertices ☐

9 marks

Challenge 3

1. Solve the riddle. What 3-D shape is it?

I have no edges.
I have no vertices.
I have one curved face.
What am I?

I am a _____

1 mark

Total: ☐ / 17 marks

Had a go ☐   **Getting there** ☐   **Got it!** ☐

Positional language

- Describe the position of objects

Position

Position simply means **where** something is. It is important to be able to describe where something is, and to understand and follow instructions to find something.

Example

Look at this kitchen scene.

The cupboards are **above** the worktop. The worktop is **below** the cupboards.

The jars are **inside** the cupboards.

The mum is to the **left** of the girl. The dad is to the **right** of the girl.

In front of the boy is a bowl. To the **left** of the bowl is a salad bowl.

A jug of juice is **on** the worktop. **Near to** the jug are salt and pepper pots.

Up on the wall, **behind** the people, are some kitchen utensils.

> **Remember**
>
> Positional language words (prepositions) can also be used for adding detail when writing about something.

> **Tip**
>
> Use words like these to describe position: above, below, left, right, near, far, over, under.

Use this picture to answer all the questions.

Challenge 1

1. Draw a sunshine in the sky. 2. Draw a ball in the sandpit.

2 marks

Challenge 2

1. Look at the picture. Use the words below to complete the sentences.

middle   behind   in   next to   right   left   above

The slide is _____ the sandpit.

There is a bucket _____ the sandpit.

The boys are playing football _____ the path.

The kite is _____ the swing.

The girl in the _____ of the playground is holding a balloon.

The see-saw is to the _____ of the sandpit.

The slide is to the _____ of the swings.

7 marks

Challenge 3

1. Write a sentence to describe where some of the children are in the picture. Use the words from Challenge 2 to help you.

_____

_____

1 mark

Total: [   ] / 10 marks

Had a go [   ]   **Getting there** [   ]   **Got it!** [   ]

Position, direction and movement

- Describe position, direction and movement, including whole, half, quarter and three-quarter turns

Position

Position means where someone or something is.

Example

Look at this picture of a farmyard.

James is in the **middle** of the farmyard.

Movement and Direction

Movement or **motion** means that someone or something is moving or travelling.

Direction is the way that something is moving. It can be used to say which way someone or something is facing. If it changes direction, then it is going somewhere else. In the picture above, James is **facing** the cow.

Turning

Turns can be measured in fractions of a turn. Look at the picture above.

- A **full turn** is a turn all the way round. If James turns around fully, he will still be facing the cow.
- Turning halfway is a **half-turn**. If James turns a half-turn he will be facing the hen.
- A **quarter turn** is also called a **right-angle turn**. If James turns a quarter turn clockwise, he will be facing the horse.
- If James turns **three quarter-turns** clockwise, he will be facing the sheep.

Remember

Turning can be seen on a clock. The hands of a clock turn 'clockwise'. If the hands turned the other way, this would be 'anti-clockwise'.

Remember

Direction can be forwards, backwards, left or right.

Tip

A full turn is like a full hour on a clock. A half turn is like half an hour on a clock. A quarter turn is a right-angle turn, like a quarter of an hour on a clock.

Key words

- turn
- clockwise
- anti-clockwise

Use this picture to answer the questions.

swings

bike

Daisy

deer

tree

Challenge 1

1. a) Which object is Daisy facing? _____

   b) Which object is behind Daisy? _____

   2 marks

Challenge 2

1. Fill in the missing words to complete the sentences.

   Daisy turns a full turn. She is facing the _____

   Daisy turns a half-turn. She is facing the _____

   Daisy turns a quarter-turn anti-clockwise.

   She is facing the _____

   3 marks

Challenge 3

1. Daisy is facing the tree.

   She turns a full turn. Then she turns a quarter-turn clockwise.

   Which object is Daisy facing now? _____

   1 mark

   Total: [ ] / 6 marks

Progress test 4

1. a) What fraction of a whole pizza is shown? Tick the correct box.

    half ☐   quarter ☐

    b) What fraction of a whole pizza is shown? Tick the correct box.

    half ☐   quarter ☐

    2 marks

2. Draw lines to match each shape to its correct description.

    8 sides

    4 corners

    6 sides

    4 equal sides

    3 corners

    1 curved side

    5 sides

    7 marks

3. a) Draw a line on each shape to split it in half. Use a ruler to help you.

    b) Draw two lines on each shape to split it into quarters. Use a ruler to help you.

    4 marks

4. Sophie sees these marbles in a shop.

She buys half of the marbles. How many does she buy?

[ ] marbles

1 mark

5. The teacher says, 'The event took place on Tuesday 18th June, 2020'.

What was the day? _____

What was the month? _____

What was the year? _____

3 marks

6. If last month was August and next month is October, what month is it now?

_____

1 mark

7. Draw lines to match the money to its value.

| £2 | £1 | 50p | 20p | 10p | 5p | 2p | 1p |

8 marks

8. a) Circle half of the mangoes.

b) Circle a quarter of the buns.

2 marks

9. **What coins would you use to pay for the toys? Tick the coin(s) you would use.**

a) £1

b) £2.50

2 marks

10. **Fill in the missing numbers.**

5   10   15   ☐   25   30   ☐   40   ☐

3 marks

11. **What time is it? Tick the correct time for the clock.**

12 o'clock ☐

8 o'clock ☐

3 o'clock ☐

1 mark

12. Read Sophie's diary entry.

Dear Diary,

Today I woke up, had my breakfast at 8 o'clock and then brushed my teeth. Then, I got my things ready for school. I had a good day at school today. When I came home in the afternoon, it was half past 3. I played with my friend Daisy at the park. After that, we both went home for tea at 5 o'clock.

a) What time did Sophie have her breakfast? _____

b) What time did Sophie get home from school? _____

c) Put the events in order from earliest to latest by writing 1, 2, 3 and 4 in the boxes. 1 is earliest. 4 is latest.

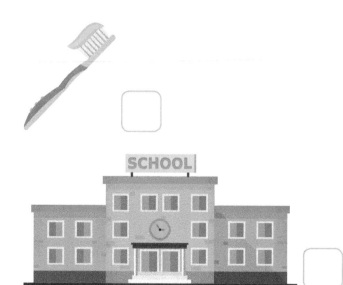  

3 marks

13. Circle the coins needed to make 96p.

1 mark

Total: ____ / 38 marks

English mixed questions

1. **Write the appropriate, correctly spelled word in each sentence.**

   a) _____ upon a time, there was a dragon.

   b) The dragon _____ called Smokey.

   c) _____ scales were green.

   d) The cave _____ still there today.

2. **Circle the correct full version of each underlined contraction.**

   a) <u>They're</u> having a party.   **They are**   **They will**

   b) <u>I'll</u> see you later.   **I will**   **I am**

   c) Wait until <u>you've</u> had lunch.   **you have**   **you will**

   d) Please <u>don't</u> make a noise.   **did not**   **do not**

   e) Soon <u>I'm</u> having tea.   **I will**   **I am**

3. **Draw lines to match each book title to what you think the book might consist of.**

The Prince and the Wizard	Stars and Planets	How to Make a Den	Puppies and Kittens

   instructions   information about pets   a fairytale   information about space

4. Read the passage and then answer the questions.

On Sunday, Lily got a ball. It was big and red.
She took it to the beach. She kicked the ball.
It went into the sea. The wind blew the ball
further and further away. Lily started to cry.

a) Who is the character in this story? _____

b) Which two words describe the ball? _____   _____

c) Where did Lily go? _____

d) What did she do to the ball? _____

e) Why do you think Lily started to cry? _____

_____

5 marks

5. Trace over the letters in each word. Then copy each word in the space provided.

horse

score

crawl

pair

dear

bear

6 marks

6. Read this short passage and answer the questions.

Sally is a school cook. She makes hot dinners for the children. Each day she cooks over one hundred meals.

Sally starts work at 8am. She chops vegetables and bakes cakes. At lunchtime, she puts the food on plates. Before she goes home, Sally washes the dishes and cleans the kitchen.

a) Where does Sally work?

_____

b) What is her job?

_____

c) How many meals does she make each day?

_____

d) What does she do before she goes home?

_____

4 marks

7. Write the correct ending for the underlined word in each sentence.

a) My dad said he was the <u>great</u>_____ footballer ever!

b) It was the <u>slow</u>_____ bus ride they had ever taken.

c) Javid has a lovely voice and is a super <u>sing</u>_____.

d) Sophie is a slow runner, but I am even <u>slow</u>_____.

4 marks

8. **Compose a sequence of three sentences for the story below.**

_____

_____

_____

_____

_____

_____

_____

_____

6 marks

9. **Write each sentence again, making sure you use capital letters and a question mark or an exclamation mark.**

a) when will we play ball

_____

b) what a super hat you are wearing

_____

c) how amazing the party was

_____

d) how old are you

_____

8 marks

10. **Write the following words in the correct sentences below.**

school	once	sea	when	our	come

a) I am in Year I at my _____.

b) I will go home _____ it is 5 o'clock.

c) Please visit us at _____ house.

d) The postman will _____ tomorrow.

e) Clara's house is by the _____.

f) We should leave at _____.

6 marks

11. **Read the text and answer the questions.**

Sabrina had never been to a rugby match before. She was smiling and couldn't stop chatting. Her heart was beating fast.

There were lots of adults and it was an adventure just to push through the forest of legs.

a) How do you think Sabrina was feeling? Which words tell you this?

_____

_____

b) What was like an adventure?

_____

_____

2 marks

12. **Re-write the underlined word from each sentence with the correct -s or -es ending.**

a) Faiza **rush** home. _____

b) Suzy **swim** fast. _____

c) Daisy **play** the flute. _____

d) Theo **wash** the car. _____

e) Put the ice cream in two **dish**. _____

5 marks

13. **Read the poem then answer the questions.**

Doctor Foster went to Gloucester,
In a shower of rain,
He stepped in a puddle,
Right up to his middle,
And never went there again.

a) Who is this poem about?

_____

b) What two things does the doctor do in the poem?

_____

_____

c) Which word is used to rhyme with rain? _____

d) Why do you think he never went to Gloucester again?

_____

4 marks

_____ Total: ☐ / 63 marks

Maths mixed questions

1. **Fill in the missing numbers.**

   104   103   102   ☐   100   99   98   ☐   ☐

   3 marks

2. **Write + (add), − (subtract) or = (equals) to make the number sentence correct.**

   15   ☐   12   ☐   3

   1 mark

PS **3. Emily has 20 sweets that she is sharing equally between her friends.**

   She puts the sweets into 4 bags. How many sweets will she put into each bag?

   ☐ sweets

   1 mark

4. **Tick the notes that make up a total value of £25.**

   £5   £10   £20

   ☐   ☐   ☐

   1 mark

5. **Tick all the squares.**

   ☐   ☐   ☐   ☐   ☐   ☐

   1 mark

6. **Fill in the missing numbers.**

   10   20   30   ☐   50   60   70   ☐   ☐

   3 marks

7. The picture shows a number bond to 20.

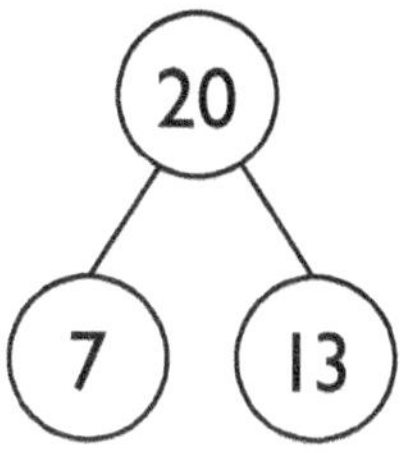

   Use this to complete the number sentences below.

   The first one has been done for you.

   20
   / \
   7   13

   | 7 | + | 13 | = | 20 |

   13 + ☐ = 20

   ☐ − 13 = 7

   20 − ☐ = 13

   ☐ 3 marks

8. Colour in one half of each of the shapes below.

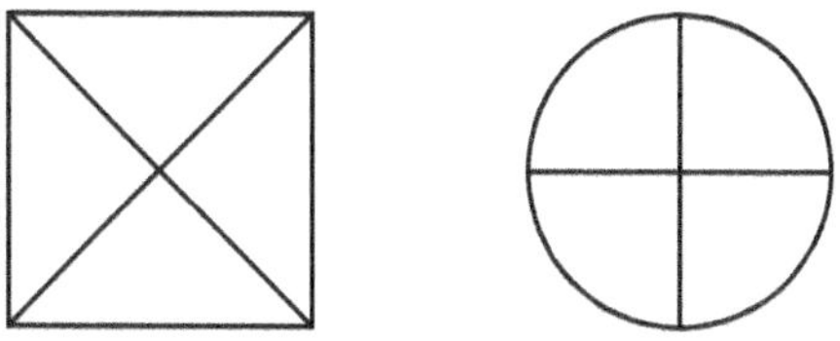

   ☐ 2 marks

9. If yesterday was Tuesday and tomorrow is Thursday, what day is it today?

   _____

   ☐ 1 mark

10. Tick the cuboid.

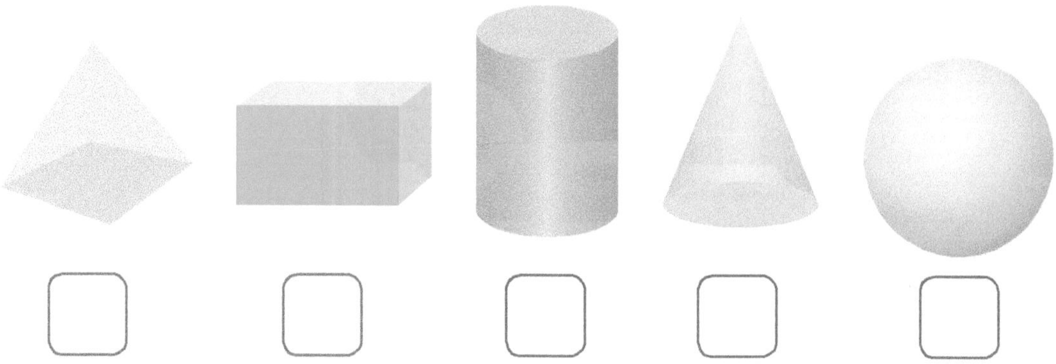

    ☐   ☐   ☐   ☐   ☐

    ☐ 1 mark

11. Write the numbers that are one less and one more than 18.

    one less ☐   18   one more ☐

    ☐ 2 marks

12. Write the missing numbers to make the number sentences correct.

a) 16 – 9 = ☐

b) 8 + 17 = ☐

13. Draw a circle around $\frac{1}{4}$ of the pennies.

14. How many minutes are there in one hour?

☐

15. Complete the sentence using one of the words below.

on   behind   under   below   outside

The car is _____ the truck.

16. Henry has 8 biscuits.   James has 10 biscuits.

Complete the sentence using one of the words below.

more   **equal**   **fewer**

James has _____ biscuits than Henry.

1 mark

17. At a bus stop, 3 people get on a bus. Nobody gets off the bus.

There are now **25** people on the bus.

How many people were on the bus to begin with?

☐ people

1 mark

18. James builds a tower out of 4 blocks.

Daisy's tower is half the size of James's tower.

How many blocks are in Daisy's tower?

☐ blocks

1 mark

19. Complete the number sentences.

a) 6 + ☐ = 10   10 − ☐ = 7

b) 15 + ☐ = 20   20 − ☐ = 14

c) 12 + 7 = ☐   18 − 9 = ☐

6 marks

113

20. Draw hands on each clock face to show the time given.

a)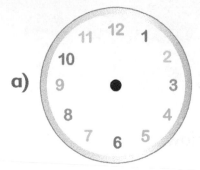

Half past 9

b)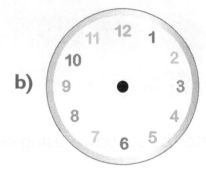

3 o'clock

c)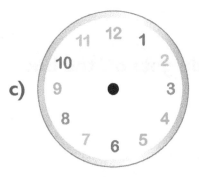

6 o'clock

d)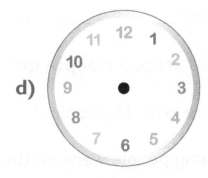

Half past 1

4 marks

21. Fill in the missing parts of the table.

Number	In words
20	
	thirteen
11	
	six

4 marks

22. Share 16 marbles between two. Draw the marbles in the circles.

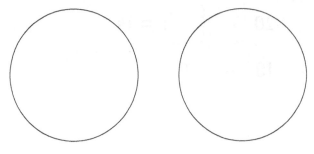

1 mark

23. Bananas come in bunches of three.

If Fabio buys 5 bunches, how many bananas will he have altogether?

☐ bananas

1 mark

24. Choose from the words below to name the 3-D shapes that are described.

sphere   **square-based pyramid**   **cone**
cube   **triangular prism**   **cylinder**

a) Has four triangular faces   _____

b) Has six square faces   _____

c) Has three faces and no vertices   _____

d) Has 1 curved face.   _____

4 marks

25. Magazines cost £1 each. Zayn buys 3 magazines. Circle the coins he will need.

2 marks

Total: ☐ /49 marks

Answers

English

Page 5
Challenge 1
1. Each word should be clearly sounded out and said aloud.
   pie, shirt, hang and play should be circled.

Challenge 2
1. a) if, up, eat
   b) tick, dog, shut

Challenge 3
1. a) soap   b) Throw
   c) bunch   d) sting

Page 7
Challenge 1
1. dragon 2, pencil 2, thunder 2, kangaroo 3

Challenge 2
1. 2 syllables: sister, Thursday, mummy, unlock
   3 syllables: Saturday, animal, unhappy, family, hospital, September

Challenge 3
1. farm, corn, popcorn 2
   jelly, pot, teapot 2
   pop, berry, blackberry 3
   black, fish, jellyfish 3
   tea, yard, farmyard 2

Page 9
Challenge 1
1. eggs, houses, chips, books, birds

Challenge 2
1. greatest, slowest, running, farmer

Challenge 3
1. 't' sound – punched, 'd' sound – played,
   'id' sound – pointed

Page 11
Challenge 1
1. a) sed – said   b) pul – pull
   c) skool – school d) frend – friend

Challenge 2
1. a) Once   b) some   c) loved   d) One

Challenge 3
1. was, is, bus, His, has, he, will, be

Page 13
Challenge 1
1. a) we have – we've   b) I am – I'm
   c) they will – they'll   d) are not – aren't

Challenge 2
1. a) didn't   b) You're   c) They're   d) isn't

Challenge 3
1. a) cannot   b) should not
   c) we are   d) I have

Page 15
Challenge 1
1. Jack and the Beanstalk – A boy called Jack
   The Smartest Giant in Town – A giant
   Puss in Boots – A cat
   The Little Red Hen – A hen

Challenge 2
1. a) Jim and Jess   b) In the cave
   c) green   d) It was snoring.

Challenge 3
1. A title which acknowledges that the story is about looking for treasure and/or that it is about the characters meeting a dragon. e.g. Jim, Jess and the Dragon or The Dragon's Treasure. The explanation should make a link between the story and the title.

Page 17
Challenge 1
1. zoo – you, shore – store, said – bed
   chip – ship, foxes – boxes, money – honey

Challenge 2
1. a) Jack and Jill   b) up the hill
   c) fetching water   d) hill

Challenge 3
1. a) a bucket
   b) head
   c) tumbling

Page 19
Challenge 1
1. How to Draw – instructions, Woodland Animals – wildlife, Cooking at Home – recipes, Sailing the World – life at sea

Challenge 2
1. a) Milk (from Sam's farm) b) Sam
   c) They are milked.

Challenge 3
1. 'You probably have milk on your breakfast cereal'. The explanation should make a link between the passage and the fact box being about the same subject (milk).

Page 21
Challenge 1
1.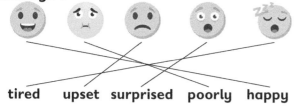

tired   upset   surprised   poorly   happy

Challenge 2
1. Any reasonable answer, e.g. He was scared of the bees.

Challenge 3
1. a) Excited – 'heart beating fast', 'wanted to shout with joy'.
   b) Any reasonable answer, e.g. there is a puppy/ there is not a puppy but a kitten.

Pages 22–25
Progress test 1: English
1. a) on, at b) but, duck, load
2. post — man   playground   2
   pan — cake   waterfall   3
   play — ground   postman   2
   water — fall   pancake   2
3. has, is, His, will, be, one
4. a) I'm b) didn't c) We're d) They're
5. a) Eva and Grandad   b) to the park
   c) fed the ducks   d) old
   e) Any reasonable answer, e.g. to share it out; so the ducks could swallow it
6. boat – vote, red – said, peel – real, hot – spot, meat – feet
7. a) Little Bo Peep   b) She has lost her sheep.
   c) sheep   d) They will come home.
8. a) in a hive   b) honey
   c) seeds   d) nectar
9. a) They will b) cannot
   c) are not   d) you have
10. a) pens   b) arches
    c) apples   d) sixes

Maths

Page 27
Challenge 1
1.

Numeral	Objects	Word
6	⚽⚽⚽⚽⚽	six
8	✏✏✏✏✏✏✏✏	eight
9	🍎🍎🍎🍎🍎🍎🍎🍎🍎	nine

Challenge 2
1. a) fourteen, 14
   b) eleven, 11
   c) thirteen, 13
   d) twelve, 12

Challenge 3
1.

1	2	3	4	5
one	two	three	four	five
6	7	8	9	10
six	seven	eight	nine	ten
11	12	13	14	15
eleven	twelve	thirteen	fourteen	fifteen
16	17	18	19	20
sixteen	seventeen	eighteen	nineteen	twenty

Page 29
Challenge 1
1. a) 1
   b) 3
   c) 7
2. a) 19
   b) 16
   c) 12

Challenge 2
1.

21	22	23	24	25	26	27	**28**	29	30
31	32	**33**	34	35	36	37	38	**39**	40
41	42	43	**44**	45	46	47	48	49	**50**

Challenge 3
1. a) 67
   b) 85
   c) 99

Page 31
Challenge 1
1. a) 6
   b) 16
2. 4, 6, 8

Challenge 2
1. a) 20
   b) 15
2. 10, 15, 20

Challenge 3
1. a) 10
   b) 40
2. 20, 30, 40

Page 33
Challenge 1
1. a) 🔵🔵🔵🔵🔵🔵 ✔
   b) ⚽⚽⚽⚽⚽⚽⚽⚽⚽ ✔
   c) ⚪⚪⚪⚪ ✔

Challenge 2
1. a) 3, 7
   b) 10, 6

Challenge 3
1. a) less
   b) less
   c) more
   d) less

Page 35
Challenge 1
1. a) 3 + 2
   b) 1 + 4
   c) 2 + 8

Challenge 2
1. a) 4, 5, 3, 2
   b) 7, 9, 6, 8
Challenge 3
1. a) +, −, +
   b) +, −, −
   c) +, +, −

Page 37
Challenge 1
1. a) 2 + 18
   b) 16 + 4
   c) 9 + 11
   d) 15 + 5

Challenge 2
1. a) 19, 20, 18
   b) 7, 3, 6

Challenge 3
1. a) +, −, +, −, +
   b) +, +, +, −, +

Page 39
Challenge 1
1. 16
2. 17

Challenge 2
1. 20, 18
2. 10, 12

Challenge 3
1. 7, 8
2. 16, 19, 11, 20, 19

Page 41
Challenge 1
1. a) 10
   b) 25
2. 10 × 5 = **50**

   6 × 2 = **12**

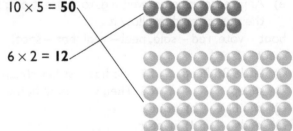

Challenge 2
1. a) 8 columns of 2 = 16
   b) 9 columns of 5 = 45

118

Challenge 3

1.

Array	Repeated addition	Multiplication
4 columns of 2	2 + 2 + 2 + 2 = 8	4 x 2 = 8
2 columns of 2	**2 + 2 = 4**	2 x 2 = 4
3 columns of 5	5 + 5 + 5 = 15	3 x 5 = 15
6 columns of 5	5 + 5 + 5 + 5 + 5 + 5 = 30	**6 x 5 = 30**
2 columns of 10	**10 + 10 = 20**	2 x 10 = 20
5 columns of 10	10 + 10 + 10 + 10 + 10 = 50	**5 x 10 = 50**

Page 43
Challenge 1

1.

2. 10, 5, 2

Challenge 2

1. 12 shared by 2 = 6

   12 shared by 4 = 3

   12 shared by 3 = 4

Challenge 3

1.

Sharing and grouping	Calculation
6 groups of 3	6 x 3
3 groups of 6	**3** x 6
18 shared by **6**	18 ÷ 6
18 shared by 3	18 ÷ **3**
18 in groups of 6	18 ÷ 6
18 in groups of **3**	18 ÷ 3

Page 45
Challenge 1

1. 12

2.  5

119

Challenge 2

1. a) 2 × 12 = 24
   b) 2 × 16 = 32

Challenge 3

1.

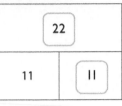

2.

24

| 12 | 12 |

Pages 46–49
Progress test 2: maths

1. a) 11, 19, 22, 30
   b) 53, 58, 61, 67
2. a) 5
   b) 10
   c) 2
3. 2, 4, 6, 8, 10, 12, 14, 16, 18, 20, 22, 24, 26, 28, 30, 32, 34, 36, 38, 40
4.

One Less	Number	One More
5	6	7
16	17	18
43	44	45
58	59	60
86	87	88
100	101	102

5. a) 3p   b) 4p   c) 5p   d) 10p
6. one, five, fourteen
7. a) 20
   b) 9
8. a) 5
   b) 5
9. 7
10. a) 20, 20, 7
    b) 6, 2, 5
11. a) 12
    b) 20
12. a) 19
    b) 8
    c) 20
13. 25
14. 50p
15. 10p
16. a) True, True, True, False
    b) James, Alice
17. 10p, 14p, 22p

English

Page 51
Challenge 1

1. Each letter should keep a consistent size and correct formation.

Challenge 2

1. Each letter should keep a consistent size, including size of ascenders and descenders, and correct formation.

Challenge 3

1. Each phrase should keep a consistent size, including size of ascenders and descenders, and correct formation.

Page 53
Challenge 1

1. Each lower-case letter should be matched correctly to its upper-case letter.

Challenge 2

1. h<u>ive</u>   sp<u>a</u>d<u>e</u>   f<u>ive</u>   b<u>one</u>

Challenge 3

1. b) <u>rain</u> a   c) <u>boat</u> o
   d) <u>night</u> i   e) <u>dream</u> e

Page 55
Challenge 1

1. Correct attempts at all five words.

Challenge 2

1. Correct attempts at all seven words.

Challenge 3

1. a) Once   b) said   c) friend

Page 57
Challenge 1
1. Discussion on meaning of each to ensure understanding that each word has an opposite meaning to the root word.
   unkind, unsafe, untidy, untrue, unhelpful

Challenge 2
1. tree**s**, hat**s**, brush**es**, apple**s**, bunch**es**, house**s**, bus**es**, boat**s**

Challenge 3
1. **a)** runs **b)** washes **c)** blows
   d) smashes **e)** flashes **f)** eats **g)** jumps
   h) munches

Page 59
Challenge 1
1. **a)** help **b)** row **c)** build **d)** look
   e) walk **f)** kick

Challenge 2
1. **a)** cook**ing** **b)** eat**ing** **c)** walk**ed**
   d) slow**est**

Challenge 3
1. wash**ing**, mix**ing**, help**ed**, eat**ing**

Page 61
Challenge 1
1. Verbal re-telling of the main events in each story.

Challenge 2
   a) Examples: nurses, doctors, police, firefighters, jobs they do, how they help
   b) Examples: the moon, stars, planets, spaceships
   c) Examples: dogs, cats, pet care

Challenge 3
1. Answers to each question. Encourage connections between each answer.

Page 63
Challenge 1
1. fairytale — The prince was saved by the princess.
   cooking — The chef prepares meals in the kitchen.
   food — (A bus can carry lots of people. / The chef prepares meals in the kitchen.)
   transport — A bus can carry lots of people.

Challenge 2
1. A complete sentence that makes sense for each idea.
   Examples: **a)** The space rocket went to the moon.
   b) Freya made new friends at her new school.

Challenge 3
1. A complete sentence that makes sense for each picture. Examples: **a)** The girl has a cute puppy.
   b) Sam was eating an ice cream.

Page 65
Challenge 1
1. 2, 3, 1

Challenge 2
1. Each sentence, verbal or written, must make sense and represent the story and related pictures.

Challenge 3
1. Correctly sequenced story re-telling.

Page 67
Challenge 1
   a) Once upon a time there was a girl called Little Red Riding Hood.
   b) At the beginning.
   c) 'Once upon a time' is used to begin stories.

Challenge 2
1. **a)** Example: The big, scary wolf followed her.
   b) Example: Soon, she arrived at Grandma's cosy, little house.

Challenge 3
1. **a)** Examples: As she walked, she **picked flowers**. As she walked, she **sang a song**.
   b) Examples: Little Red Riding Hood **knocked on the door**. Little Red Riding Hood **let herself in**.

Page 69
Challenge 1
1. **a)** **M**y bike is fast. **b)** **T**he tree is tall.
   c) **I**t is a sunny day.

Challenge 2
1. **a)** ⓦe went to the shop. ⓜum got a new dress.
   b) ⓓad was making lunch. ⓗe is a good cook.

Challenge 3
1. **I**t was a hot day. **T**he dog was hot. **T**he girl was hot.
   The girl jumped in the water. **T**he dog jumped in the water.

Challenge 1
1. a) **M**y name is **F**red.
   b) **W**e are visiting **S**am.
   c) **O**n **S**unday, they went swimming.

Challenge 2
   a) ⓞn ⓕriday, we went to ⓦales.
   b) ⓐt school, ⓘ saw ⓐnna.
   c) ⓛeila went to ⓛondon with ⓙess.

Challenge 3
   a) **M**y friend **J**ack has a big house. **H**e lives in **P**aris in **F**rance.
   b) **O**n **M**ondays, **I** play the flute. My teacher is called **H**elen.

Page 73
Challenge 1
1. a) <u>What</u> is your name?
   b) <u>How</u> old are you?
   c) <u>Where</u> do you live?
   d) <u>When</u> is your birthday?

Challenge 2
1. a) ✔ d) ✔ e) ✔ f) ✔

Challenge 3
1. Examples:
   a) What is your name?
   b) What time is it?
   c) What is your favourite fruit?
   d) Where are you from?

Page 75
Challenge 1
1. a) What a fantastic sunset that was!
   b) How amazing your painting is!
   c) What brilliant trainers you are wearing!
   d) How incredible that cake tastes!

Challenge 2
1. b) ✔ d) ✔ f) ✔

Challenge 3
1. a) Examples: it was! it is!
   b) Examples: looked! tasted!
   c) Examples: was! is!
   d) Examples: show it had been! view it was!

Page 77
Challenge 1
1. a) Dev plays chess **and** he is best in his class.
   b) Flo's favourite flavour of crisps is cheese **and** onion.
   c) The hill is steep **and** it has lots of trees.

Challenge 2
1. a) Lucy has a dog and it is called Sandy.
   b) The shop is big and it sells most things.
   d) I am in Year 1 and my teacher is Mr Jones.

Challenge 3
1. a) Example: They saw the swimming pool **and jumped in.**
   b) Example: I went to see my cousin **and we played on bikes.**
   c) Example: Mum likes to bake cakes **and they are very tasty.**

Pages 78–81
Progress test 3: English
1. **M**onday, **Tues**day, **Wed**nesday, **Thurs**day, **Fri**day, **Satur**day, **Sun**day
2. a) fast**er** b) play**ing** c) quiet**er** d) paint**ing**
3. a) Example: There is a cat in the tree.
   b) Example: The girl is riding a bike.
4. a) Jane   b) big, green
   c) She likes meeting people.   d) school, home
5. Jane has been a bus driver for 15 years. ✔
6. 2, 3, 1
7. The tiger was exciting. ✔
8. a) **I**t is sunny outside. **W**e will play in the garden.
   b) **J**ames goes to church every Sunday. He loves it.
   c) **M**y friend **R**ishi lives in **I**ndia.
   d) **T**he dog is called **T**oby. **I**t belongs to **S**ophie.
9. a) The snow is cold.   b) It is a red ball.
   c) My kite is green.   d) Her sister is Emma.
10. a) Examples: different types of food, where it comes from
    b) Examples: sandcastles, the sea, rockpools
    c) Examples: animals, tractors, the farmer

Maths

Page 83
Challenge 1
1.

2. Half the square coloured in; half the triangle coloured in. Examples:

Challenge 2

1. Examples:

Challenge 3

1. 2 bananas circled; 4 apples circled

2. b) ✔ **c)** ✔

Page 85
Challenge 1

1.

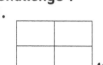 ✔   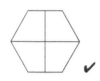 ✔

2. One quarter of the square coloured in; one quarter of the circle coloured in. Examples:

Challenge 2

1. Examples:

 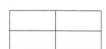

Challenge 3

1. 1 banana circled; 2 apples circled

2. a) ✔ **c)** ✔

Page 87
Challenge 1

1. a) 7 **b)** 4 **c)** 12

Challenge 2

1. a) Wednesday
b) Friday
c) Tuesday
d) Saturday

Challenge 3

1. a) February **b)** April
c) November **d)** June

Page 89
Challenge 1

1. a)  ✔

b) ✔

Challenge 2

1. one o'clock, half past five, seven o'clock, half past eleven

Challenge 3

1.

Page 91
Challenge 1

1. a) 5 **b)** 4 **c)** 3

Challenge 2

1. a) 2p **b)** £2 **c)** 5p
d) 50p **e)** 1p **f)** £1

Challenge 3

1. 1p, 2p, 5p, 10p, 20p, 50p, £1, £2

Page 93
Challenge 1

1.

rectangle square octagon hexagon circle triangle pentagon

Challenge 2

1. Circle 1, 0
Triangle 3, 3
Rectangle 4, 4
Pentagon 5, 5
Hexagon 6, 6

Challenge 3

1. square

Page 95

Challenge 1

1.
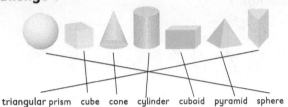

triangular prism · cube · cone · cylinder · cuboid · pyramid · sphere

Challenge 2

1. Cuboid 6, 12, 8
   Cylinder 3, 2, 0
   Square-based pyramid 5, 8, 5

Challenge 3

1. sphere

Page 97

Challenge 1

1. sunshine drawn in the sky
2. ball drawn in the sandpit

Challenge 2

1. The slide is **behind** the sandpit.
   There is a bucket **in** the sandpit.
   The boys are playing football **next to** the path.
   The kite is **above** the swing.
   The girl in the **middle** of the playground is holding a balloon.
   The see-saw is to the **right** of the sandpit.
   The slide is to the **left** of the swings.

Challenge 3

1. Examples: The children are in the playground / in the sandpit / on the see-saw / on the swing / on the path / next to the swing / next to the slide.

Page 99

Challenge 1

1. a) tree
   b) swings

Challenge 2

1. a) tree
   b) swings
   c) deer

Challenge 3

1. bike

Pages 100–103

Progress test 4: maths

1. a) half
   b) quarter

2.
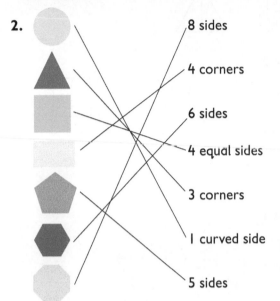

8 sides
4 corners
6 sides
4 equal sides
3 corners
1 curved side
5 sides

3. a) Examples:
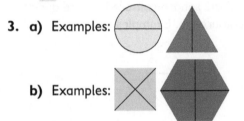

   b) Examples:

4. 10
5. a) Tuesday
   b) June
   c) 2020
6. September
7.
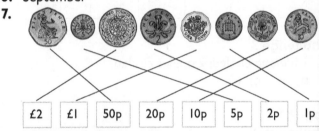

£2 | £1 | 50p | 20p | 10p | 5p | 2p | 1p

8. a) 9 mangoes circled
   b) 4 buns circled
9. a) £1 ✔
   b) £2 ✔ 50p ✔
10. 20, 35, 45
11. 3 o'clock

12. a) 8 o'clock
  b) half past 3
  c) 2

 4

3  1

13.

Pages 104–109
English mixed questions
1. a) Once **b)** was **c)** His/Her/Its **d)** is
2. a) They are **b)** I will **c)** you have
  d) do not **e)** I am
3. *The Prince and the Wizard* – a fairytale, *Stars and Planets* – information about space, *How to Make a Den* – instructions, *Puppies and Kittens* – information about pets
4. a) Lily **b)** big, red **c)** to the beach
  d) kicked it **e)** The ball had gone. She might not get it back.
5. All letters to be correctly formed and of consistent size.
6. a) At school (or in the kitchen/school kitchen)
  b) (school) cook **c)** over one hundred
  d) washes the dishes and cleans the kitchen
7. a) est **b)** est **c)** er **d)** er
8. Each sentence must make sense and represent the related pictures with correct punctuation. Examples: The rocket went into space. It landed on the planet Zeg. The astronaut met an alien.
9. a) When will we play ball?
  b) What a super hat you are wearing!
  c) How amazing the party was!
  d) How old are you?
10. a) school **b)** when **c)** our **d)** come
  e) sea **f)** once
11. a) Excited. She was smiling, chatting and her heart was beating fast.
  b) Pushing through the people.
12. a) rushes **b)** swims **c)** plays
  d) washes **e)** dishes
13. a) Doctor Foster **b)** He went to Gloucester. He stepped in a puddle. **c)** again **d)** Any reasonable answer such as: He didn't like it there because he stood in a deep puddle.

Pages 110–115
Maths mixed questions
1. 101, 97, 96
2. –, =
3. 5
4. £5 note ✔ £20 note ✔
5.

  ✔ ✔ ✔

6. 40, 80, 90
7. 7, 20, 7
8. Examples: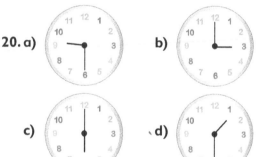
9. Wednesday
10. ✔
11. 17, 19
12. a) 7 **b)** 25
13. 2 pennies circled.
14. 60
15. on
16. more
17. 22
18. 2
19. a) 4, 3 **b)** 5, 6 **c)** 19, 9

20. a) [clock] **b)** [clock]
  c) [clock] **d)** [clock]

21.

Number	In Words
20	**twenty**
13	thirteen
11	**eleven**
6	six

22.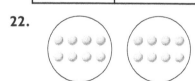
23. 15
24. a) square-based pyramid **b)** cube
  c) cylinder **d)** sphere
25. £1 coin and £2 coin circled.

125

Glossary

English

Adjective   A describing word; a word used to describe things such as colour, size or other features of an object or person.

Apostrophe   ' A punctuation mark used to replace missing letters in contracted words, e.g. I am – I'm.

Ascender   The part of a letter that rises above the main part of the letter, e.g. b, d and h.

Capital letter   A letter of the alphabet written in a larger and often different form than the corresponding letter, e.g. A a B b C c.

Compound word   A word made by combining two words into one, e.g. play + ground = playground, post + man = postman.

Comprehension   Understanding of a text.

Contraction   A word made from shortening two words and replacing the missing letters with an apostrophe, e.g. I am ⟶ I'm.

Descender   The part of a letter that extends below the main part of the letter, e.g. g, p and y.

Exception word   A word that does not follow a spelling rule or cannot be easily sounded out when segmented.

Exclamation mark   ! A punctuation mark that comes at the end of an exclamation sentence, e.g. What an amazing view!

Fiction   A made-up story.

Full stop   . A punctuation mark that comes at the end of a sentence.

Inference   Using clues in a text to decide how or why something has happened, or how and why a character acts or feels a certain way.

Joining word   A word used to join two words or two clauses, e.g. 'and'.

Letter   A symbol used to show a sound or part of a word. Part of the alphabet, e.g. a, b, c, d, e, f, etc.

Lower-case   Letters in their most common form (e.g. a, b, c, d) and not capital letters.

Narrative   A piece of writing made from a sequence of related sentences.

Non-fiction   Writing using facts, e.g. information texts.

Noun   A word used to name a person, place or thing.

Plan   An idea for a piece of writing, which shows what the main points will be and the parts it will be organised into.

Plural   More than one of something, e.g. trees, foxes.

Poem   A type of writing that describes something or tells a story, often using rhyming words or repeating words.

Prediction   Working out what may happen next in a text, usually by thinking about what has already happened and using clues from that.

Prefix   A letter or letters added to the beginning of a root word which changes the word meaning.

Proofread   Reading through writing to check for sense and mistakes.

Punctuation   Helps the reader recognise things such as the beginning (capital letter) and end of a sentence (full stop, question mark, exclamation mark) or other grammatical features such as an apostrophe for shortened words (e.g. can't, I'm, they'll).

Question   A sentence used to ask something. Questions often start with the words: what, where, when, who, how or why. They end with a question mark.

Question mark   ? A punctuation mark that comes at the end of a question, e.g. What is the time?

Rhyme   Two or more words where the final sound sounds the same, e.g. fish, dish.

Root word   A word which has meaning on its own but can also have prefixes, suffixes or both added to change the meaning.

Sentence   A group of words that give information and which begin with a capital letter, contain an action word and end with a suitable punctuation mark.

Sequence   A group of sentences or ideas that are spoken or written in order.

Singular   One of something, e.g. apple, he, she, tree.

Sound   A part of a spoken word made from a single letter or a combination of letters.

Spelling rule   A pattern of letters that is found in several different words.

Suffix   A letter or letters added to the end of a root word which changes the word meaning.

Syllable   A 'beat' in a word. Each syllable contains a vowel sound.

Upper-case   Capital letters, e.g. A, B, C, D.

Verb   An action word or 'doing word', e.g. read, swim, bake.

Vowel   The letters a, e, i, o and u.

Word   A group of letters which together have a meaning.

Maths

2-D shapes   Shapes that are flat, having only 2 dimensions – height/length and width.

3-D shapes   Shapes that have a solid form, having 3 dimensions – height/length, width and depth.

Addition   Finding the total value of two or more numbers. Represented by the symbol +.

Array   A picture showing multiplication and division as columns of dots or symbols. For example, 2 x 3 could be shown as 2 columns of 3 dots.

Calculation   Working out the amount or number of something.

Circle   A 2-D shape with no corners.

Clockwise and anti-clockwise   A way of indicating the direction of a turn. Clockwise involves a turn to the right, as if following the hands of a clock; anti-clockwise involves a turn to the left, against or opposite to the direction of a clock's hands.

Cone   A 3-D shape with 2 faces (1 circular), 1 edge and 1 vertex.

Cube   A 3-D shape with 6 square faces, 12 edges and 8 vertices.

Cuboid   A 3-D shape with 6 faces, 4 or all of which are rectangular, 12 edges and 8 vertices.

Currency   A system of money – the UK's currency is pounds and pence.

Cylinder   A 3-D shape with 2 circular faces, 1 rectangular face, 2 edges and no vertices.

Division   The process of dividing a number up into equal parts and finding how many equal parts can be made. It is represented by the symbol ÷.

Edge   The place on a 3-D shape where 2 faces meet.

Equals   The same amount or number.

Even numbers   Numbers that always end with 0, 2, 4, 6 or 8.

Face   Any surface of a 3-D shape. Faces can be flat 2-D shapes, or even curved like in cones and spheres.

Fraction   A number which represents part of a whole, e.g. half $\frac{1}{2}$ or a quarter $\frac{1}{4}$.

Grouping   A way of dividing and sharing a total number of objects into equal groups. (This is different to sharing where a number of objects are continually shared out.)

Hexagon   A 2-D shape with 6 sides and 6 corners.

Multiplication   Lots of, or 'times by'. Multiplication is repeated addition – it is like adding the same number lots of times. It is represented by the symbol '**x**' in number sentences.

Numeral   A number digit rather than the word, e.g. 1, 2, 3.

Number facts/bonds   Pairs of numbers that add up to a specific number. For example, the number bonds to 10 are 10 + 0, 9 + 1, 8 + 2 and so on. They also show patterns that are repeated for other number bonds, for example to 20 or 100.

Number line   A visual representation of numbers along a horizontal line. Can start at 0 or represent a set of numbers from elsewhere in the number system. Used to support counting, place value and calculation skills.

Number square   A set of numbers written in sequence in a square format, often from 1 to 100.

Odd numbers   All whole numbers that are not exactly divisible by 2. Odd numbers always end in 1, 3, 5, 7 or 9.

Octagon   A 2-D shape with 8 sides and 8 corners.

Operation   The 4 mathematical operations are addition, subtraction, multiplication and division.

Ordering   Putting numbers in the correct order according to size. Ascending order goes smallest to largest; descending order from largest to smallest.

Pentagon   A 2-D shape with 5 sides and 5 corners.

Prism   A 3-D shape with flat sides and identically shaped end faces. The cross section of a prism is the same all the way through. Examples are a triangular prism and a hexagonal prism.

Pyramid (square-based)   A 3-D shape with 4 triangular faces, 1 square face and 5 vertices.

Pyramid (triangular-based)   A 3-D shape with 4 triangular faces and 4 vertices.

Repeated addition   A way of teaching about multiplication as the repeated grouping of the same number. For example, 4 x 2 is the same as four groups of 2, or 2 + 2 + 2 + 2.

Sharing   A way of dividing by splitting up and sharing a total number of objects out. (This is different to grouping where a total number of objects are grouped.)

Sphere   A 3-D shape with 1 curved face, no edges and no vertices.

Subtraction   Taking 1 number away from another, finding the difference between them. Represented by the symbol −.

Triangle   A 2-D shape with 3 straight sides and 3 corners.

Turns   Movements in a space, either clockwise or anti-clockwise.

Vertex   The place (corner) on a 3-D shape where faces meet. (Plural = vertices.)

Acknowledgements

The authors and publisher are grateful to the copyright holders for permission to use quoted materials and images.
All images are ©Shutterstock.com and ©HarperCollins*Publishers*
All facts are correct at time of going to press.
Published by Collins
An imprint of HarperCollins*Publishers*
1 London Bridge Street
London SE1 9GF

HarperCollins*Publishers*
Macken House, 39/40 Mayor Street Upper,
Dublin 1, D01 C9W8, Ireland

ISBN: 978-0-00-839877-4
First published 2020
10 9 8 7
©HarperCollins*Publishers* Ltd. 2020

Authors: Jon Goulding and Brad Thompson
Publisher: Fiona McGlade
Project Development: Katie Galloway
Cover Design: Kevin Robbins and Sarah Duxbury
Inside Concept Design: Ian Wrigley
Page Layout: Q2A Media
Production: Karen Nulty
Printed in the United Kingdom

MIX
Paper
FSC™ C007454

Progress charts

Use these charts to record your results in the four Progress Tests. Colour in the questions that you got right to help you identify any areas that you might need to study and practise again. (These areas are indicated in the 'See page...' row in the charts.)

Progress test 1: English

	Q1	Q2	Q3	Q4	Q5	Q6	Q7	Q8	Q9	Q10	TOTAL /47
See page...	54	58	62	18	18	14	20	62	68	60	

Progress test 2: Maths

	Q1	Q2	Q3	Q4	Q5	Q6	Q7	Q8	Q9	Q10	Q11	Q12	Q13	Q14	Q15	Q16	Q17	TOTAL /52
See page...	26	38	28	32	44	26	38	34	38	38	38	28	40	40	42	32	44	

Progress test 3: English

	Q1	Q2	Q3	Q4	Q5	Q6	Q7	Q8	Q9	Q10	TOTAL /48
See page...	54	58	62	18	18	14	20	62	68	60	

Progress test 4: Maths

	Q1	Q2	Q3	Q4	Q5	Q6	Q7	Q8	Q9	Q10	Q11	Q12	Q13	TOTAL /38
See page...	82/84	92	82/84	82	86	86	90	82/84	90	30	88	86	90	

Use this table to record your results for the Mixed questions sections on pages 104–115.

English mixed questions	Total score:	/ 63 marks
Maths mixed questions	Total score:	/ 49 marks

128